Alternative Dispute Resolution

LEGAL PRACTICE COURSE

WITHDRAWN

WP 2180658 6

Alternative Dispute Resolution

Paul Newman

Barrister
Gray's Inn, London
Senior Construction Lawyer
and member of CEDR
Construction Industry Working Group

UNIVERSITY OF WOLVERHAMPTON
LIBRARY

Acc No. 2180658 CLASS 321

347,

CONTROL 1858111706 09

DATE 20 SEP 1999 SITE WL NEW

CLT Professional Publishing Ltd
A Division of Central Law Group

© Paul Newman 1999

Published by CLT Professional Publishing Ltd
A member of the Central Law Group
31-33 Stonehills House
Welwyn Garden City
Hertfordshire
AL8 6PU

ISBN 1 85811 170 6

All rights reserved. No part of this publication may be reproduced, stored in a retrieval
system, or transmitted, in any form or by any means, electronic, mechanical, photocopying,
recording or otherwise, without the prior permission of the publisher.
The moral right of the author has been asserted.

Typeset by Heath Lodge Publishing Services

Printed in Great Britain by The Book Company Ltd

Contents

Table of Cases

Preface

In 1990, ADR was a complete unknown to me. Encouraged by a colleague, and fellow court construction lawyer, who had worked in Hong Kong and seen ADR at first hand, I attended my first mediation training course. I returned enthused, seeing ADR as self evidently sensible in terms of cost savings, speed and reducing stress on the participants. During the greater part of this decade I have striven hard to promote ADR and raise its profile. I hope this book will aid the process. ADR has thrived in parts of the world, inspired perhaps by social or religious norms that pervade those societies. The same imperatives may be lacking in the United Kingdom, requiring the development of different reasons to espouse ADR. Perhaps the "culture change" is required from grass roots in schools and colleges. Much litigation is based on an unwillingness to lose face when things have gone wrong. For employees there are infrequently rewards for admitting they are human.

My thanks go, as usual, to a long suffering publisher who has endured with patience the various delays, my wife, Veronica, who has taken on more than her fair share of the household decorating, and my original colleague, Gil Crocker, who promoted the initial interest in ADR, and those bodies and institutions which have consented to the reproduction of their materials in the appendices.

Paul Newman, February 1999

Chapter 1

Arbitration Litigation and the Emergence of Alternative Dispute Resolution

A former Chief Justice of the United States of America, Warren Burger, once said:

> "The obligation of our profession is ... to serve as healers of human conflict. To fulfil our traditional obligation means that we should provide mechanisms that can produce an acceptable result in the shortest possible time, with the least possible expense and with the minimum of stress on the participants. That is what justice is all about."[1]

Leaving to one side the possibly conflicting emotions of those involved in the dispute resolution business, where certain lawyers need to question the value of a "litigation client who is not litigating", no sensible person could dissent from Warren Burger's comments. Dispute resolution is a service industry and must recognise client needs. This theme has been taken up by many leading members of the judiciary and was the cornerstone of Lord Woolf's interim and final reviews of civil litigation[2], *Access to Justice*. Another very senior judge, the former Lord Chief Justice, Lord Taylor, rightly said in identifying the obligation of the legal profession to be responsible in plying its trade:

> "A trial is not a game. The role of a judge should not be restricted to that of an umpire sitting well above the play, intervening only to restrain intemperate language and racket throwing."[3]

---

1 Robert Coulson, *Professional Mediation of Civil Disputes*, American Arbitration Association, 1984, pp. 6–7
2 *Final Report to the Lord Chancellor on the Civil Justice System in England and Wales, Lord Woolf*, July 1996, *Interim Report to the Lord Chancellor on the Civil Justice System in England and Wales*, Lord Woolf, HMSO, June 1995
3 Quoted by Lord Alexander of Weedon QC in *Training Lawyers – Healers or Hired Guns?* Child & Co Lecture, 15th March 1995, p. 3

Lord Taylor's remark echoed earlier words of Warren Burger who on one occasion said:

> "Trials by the adversarial contest must in time go the way of ancient trial by battle and blood".[4]

Increasingly, litigation, the legal process and the ways of lawyers and expert witnesses have attracted a very poor press. Particularly in the United States lawyers are the butt of savage jokes which emphasise their reputed avarice and self interest. Even in the United Kingdom, when the City law firm, Herbert Smith, surveyed the top 400 companies in *The Times Top 1000* for their views on litigation, the lawyers found widespread criticism of the length, complexity and cost of civil justice:

> "A substantial majority (70%) suggested the whole system takes too long, whilst almost 40% suggested that the costs of litigation are far too high."[5]

Companies apparently support a shift away from oral advocacy in civil trials and a greater emphasis on written submissions. They want judges, not the parties to the dispute, to control the pace of proceedings and to determine how long cases should take. More than 60% of the firms questioned favoured a paper trial instead of one based on oral argument and evidence; and a substantial majority wanted control of the timetable of cases given to a *procedural judge*.

Over the years various "captains of industry" have criticised the legal process. For instance, Ian Dixon, Chairman of Wilmott Dixon and the then Chairman of the Construction Industry Council, was quoted on one occasion as saying:

> "You can't win if you go to court. The high legal costs are part of it. Litigation is long and repetitive. The legal system is abysmal and inefficient."[6]

Arbitration, traditionally promoted by its proponents as a *no nonsense* method of dispute resolution, relying more on technical assessment than on the application of judicial nuances, has for a number of years been regarded as legalistic. In *Northern Regional Health Authority v Derek Crouch Construction Company Ltd*, overruled by the House of Lords in 1998 on other grounds, Sir John

---

4 *ibid.* p. 5
5 *The Times*, January 1995
6 *Building*, 7th February 1992, p. 9

Donaldson MR stated that "arbitration is usually no more and no less than litigation in the private sector".[7]

Similarly overseas, the conclusion reached in an Australian research report into claims and disputes in the construction industry, *Strategies for the Reduction of Claims and Disputes in the Construction Industry – a Research Report* (various authors), was that:

> "... arbitration has broken down as a cheap and efficient means of resolving construction disputes, albeit that the cause may be the strenuously adversarial manner in which the disputants themselves pursue the arbitral process."[8]

Whether or not the Arbitration Act 1996 will improve the position and rehabilitate arbitration as a cost effective means of resolving commercial disputes time will tell.

The Arbitration Act 1996, the purpose of which is to breathe fresh life into arbitration, had a long period of gestation. The Departmental Advisory Committee (DAC), latterly with governmental involvement, produced two draft Bills, the second of which went out to public consultation in July 1995. The aim was to restate English arbitration law in clear and *user-friendly* language. Some commentators supported the incorporation into English law of the UNCITRAL Model Law as had occurred in Scotland a few years earlier. Decisions of the English courts, exercising their supervisory jurisdiction, had caused disquiet amongst foreign parties who chose London for their arbitration. The promoters of new English legislation decided that although the UNCITRAL Model Law had many useful lessons, English law and practice were too well developed by case law precedents to justify the wholescale adoption of the Model Law. The exercise became one of consolidating the Arbitration Acts 1950–1979, modernising their language and inserting apposite features from the Model Law.

The preamble to the Act states:-

> "An Act to restate and improve the law relating to arbitration pursuant to an arbitration agreement; to make other provision relating to arbitration and arbitration awards; and for connected purposes."

Much of the dissatisfaction with English arbitration law and practice came from foreign users of the system who found the supervisory jurisdiction and interventionist tendencies of the English courts both irksome and unexpected. Illustrative of the problem was

---

7 [1984] 1 QB 644, at 670
8 Australian Federation of Construction Contractors

Coppée-Lavalin SA/NV v Ken-Ren Chemicals and Fertilisers Ltd. [9] The House of Lords held by a majority that the English courts did have jurisdiction to order security for costs in an arbitration governed by the ICC Arbitration Procedure albeit that the case had no connection whatsoever with England and Wales beyond the fact that the case was to be heard in London.

A primary objective of the new legislation has been to enhance the powers of arbitrators and guarantee party autonomy, albeit subject to the supervisory jurisdiction of the English courts whose purpose will be to assist arbitration rather than suffocate its operation. Section 1 sets out the overriding principles behind Part 1:

> "The provisions of this Part are founded on the following principles, and shall be construed accordingly -
> (a) the object of arbitration is to obtain the fair resolution of disputes by an impartial tribunal without unnecessary delay or expense;
> (b) the parties shall be free to agree how their disputes are resolved, subject only to such safeguards as are necessary in the public interest;
> (c) in matters governed by this Part, the court should not intervene except as provided by this Part"

Section 33 of the 1996 Act emphasises that the tribunal must:

- act fairly and impartially as between the parties (*i.e.* apply the rules of natural justice)
- adopt procedures suitable to the circumstances, which avoid unnecessary delay and expense.

Arbitrators are not to behave necessarily as if they were High Court judges and should proceed, as appropriate, on a "documents only" or "look sniff" basis.

The key powers for the conduct of references are set out in Section 34 of the 1996 Act. Among the more important are sub-sections (2)(c), (d), (e), (f), (g) and (h). Sub-section (2)(c) relates to written statements of claim and defence rather than conventional pleadings, which have long been widespread in arbitration. These statements comprise the analysis of the legal issues, the evidence by which these are to be proved, and copy documents or extracts from documents upon which the parties rely. Over recent times the judges have criticised the extent to which litigation parties indulge in discovery and the purpose of (d) is to limit severely the current tendency to blanket discovery and inspection.

Sub-paragraphs (e) and (g) are important powers. They permit the tribunal to take the lead in establishing the facts and essentially provide for an inquisitorial approach. There has been a great debate in case law concerning the extent to which an arbitrator may act inquisitorially. Continental Europe has used an inquisitorial system for generations. Under such a system the judge or arbitrator is investigative. He is not there merely to assess the evidence having allowed each party to produce its evidence and cross-examine the opponent's witnesses (sometimes extremely crossly). As a general principle, adversarial methods mean more lengthy hearings and a lesser reliance upon documentation. Lord Justice Kerr (as he then was) said on one occasion:

> "Arbitrators should not allow themselves to be dominated by English procedure. In long complex cases the Continental inquisitorial procedure is often more effective than our adversarial system. It is often better for the Tribunal to limit discovery in the first instance; to appoint its own expert, and then to exercise control over the volume of discovery and the witnesses whom it wants to hear. Our arbitrators will have to be more imaginative than to follow the mirror image of the procedure in our courts."[10]

In *Carlisle Place Investments Ltd* v *Wimpey Construction (UK) Ltd*[11] Robert Goff J said:

> "I know of no requirement that an arbitrator must allow each party to call all the evidence which he wishes to call. It must depend on the circumstances of the particular case whether or not the arbitrator decides, in exercise of his discretion, to conduct the arbitration in a particular way."[12]

However, the trend of legal authority, such as it is, appears to have been prior to the Arbitration Act 1996 against arbitrators adopting an inquisitorial approach. Albeit that it was not a commercial arbitration but one under the special provisions in the County Court, in *Chilton* v *Saga Holidays plc*[13] an arbitration award by a County Court Registrar was set aside on the grounds that in England and Wales courts and arbitrators operate on an adversarial basis. In *Town and City Properties (Development) Ltd* v *Wiltshier Southern Ltd & Another*[14], an arbitration on interim certificates under a

---

10 Quoted in *Handbook of Arbitration Practice* (2nd edn), ed. Bernstein and Wood, Sweet & Maxwell, 1993, p. 60, 61, but not in Handbook of Arbitration Practice (3rd edition), ed. Bernstein, Tackaberry, Marriott, Wood, Sweet & Maxwell, 1998. Perhaps the editors considered the Arbitration Act 1996 rendered this quotation redundant.
11 (1980) 15 BLR 109
12 at 117
13 [1986] 1 AER 841
14 (1988) 44 BLR 109

building contract, the arbitrator conducted an inquisitorial procedure with the expert witnesses although the claimant had requested a full hearing with traditional cross-examination. The arbitrator was subsequently removed for misconduct under section 23(1) Arbitration Act 1950 because he had chosen to conduct the proceedings in an inquisitorial manner.

Again, sub-section (2)(f) will be of interest both to lawyers and arbitrators in that arbitrators are now expressly permitted to dispense with the strict rules of evidence if appropriate in all the circumstances. The ability of the tribunal to act inquisitorially is further assisted by section 37 of the 1996 Act. The tribunal can, unless otherwise agreed, appoint experts or legal advisors to report to it and the parties, or to appoint assessors to assist on technical matters.

Section 38 of the 1996 Act details a number of powers which may be used as part of the arbitration process. An important one is found in section 38(3) which permits the tribunal to award security for costs, perhaps not necessarily adopting the same criteria as would be used in the courts. Under sub-section (4) the tribunal may give directions in regard to particular property, *e.g.* preservation orders, *etc.*

A major defect with arbitration has been the absence of any effective interlocutory relief, particularly on principles which equate with the granting of summary judgment or interim payments in the High Court or County Court. This situation is partly redressed by section 39 of the Act which, provided the parties agree, empowers the tribunal to make provisional orders including ones for the payment of money. Section 39 could not be used to permit an arbitrator to grant a Mareva Injunction or an Anton Pillar Order. Under the 1950 Act, unless any incorporated arbitration rules specifically permit such an award, the only possibility is an interim award which is a final award on the issues to which it relates.

Certain default powers are contained in section 41 of the 1996 Act, which are applicable except in the event of agreement to the contrary. First, sub-section (3) contains the statutory reversal of the much criticised decision of the House of Lords in *Bremer Vulcan Schiffbau und Maschinenfabrik v South India Shipping Corporation*,[15] where the House of Lords held that an arbitrator could not dismiss claims for want of prosecution. In fact, this section is itself a re-enactment of section 13A of the 1950 Act which was inserted by section 102 of the Courts and Legal Services Act 1990. In addition, section 41 provides scope for the arbitrator to proceed in

---

the absence of a party and sets out various provisions relating to temporary orders. Section 42 allows recourse to the courts to uphold temporary orders made by the tribunal and includes the possibility of an application being made by the tribunal itself. Other support powers of the courts are found in sections 43, 44 and 45; the last mentioned permits the court to decide preliminary issues of law.

Time will tell whether the 1996 Act will be as rigid and legalistic in its operation as the 1950–1979 Acts have been. First, there are the general powers under section 34, already discussed, to operate on an inquisitorial basis. Second, section 46 (closely modelled on Article 28 of the Model Law) permits the arbitrator to act, with the consent of the parties, as an *amiable compositeur* and reach decisions *ex aequo et bono*. The extent to which this allows the parties to contract out of the principles of natural justice is debatable given the tribunal's general duties under section 33 of the Act. Third, there is some debate as to the interpretation to be placed on section 48 of the Act. Sub-section (1) states:

> "The parties are free to agree on the powers exercisable by the arbitral tribunal as regards remedies."

Subject to further definition by the courts, it is arguable that the word, "remedies", as used in sub-section (1), permits the parties to agree that the solution imposed by the arbitrator may extend beyond those available at law.

Perhaps the lawyers' apparent inability to resolve disputes efficiently and cost-effectively stems partly from the way in which we train our lawyers and the alacrity with which many expert witnesses become part of the legal process as well as from the average client's tendency to place *wants* above *reality*. Ours may be an adversarial system of law, but the words of a President of Columbia University are significant:

> "The idea that we should spent all our time in law school teaching people how to win instead of how to settle is very damaging".[16]

It is however important to strike a balance in any assessment of litigation and arbitration and to resist the temptation of concluding that they are never successful or in a client's best interests. Alternative Dispute Resolution (ADR) is not a panacea but an additional tool in the litigator's armoury. On occasions, a claimant is pursuing outstanding monies from an unprincipled opponent who has no intention of negotiating sensibly. Frequently facts are complex and

---

16 Quoted by Lord Alexander of Weedon QC, op.cit.n.3, p. 21

can justifiably produce different but ostensibly valid interpretations. Less often cases throw up points of contract interpretation and an analysis of legal principles is necessary. Litigation, including summary judgment under RSC Order 14 and interim payments under RSC Order 29, have been an extremely effective means of debt collecting where the issues are factually or legally clear-cut, although the coming into force of section 9 of the Arbitration Act 1996 (mandatory stay of proceedings where there is an arbitration clause in the contract) has removed the possibility of summary judgment or an interim payment under contracts where the arbitration provision has not been deleted in favour of litigation.

However, many commercial disputes do not lend themselves to litigation or arbitration. The issues are not clearly delineated; a fact well known to the parties (at least if they are honest with themselves) and one which some lawyers appear to ignore for as long as possible. It is sometimes claimed that litigation or arbitration provide a *lever* on the defendant to make him negotiate and enhance the prospects of a quicker negotiated settlement. Such a tactic often fails. The parties become more and more entrenched in the litigation until the dispute is resolved by way of a belated piece of *horse-trading*. This happens only when high legal costs have been incurred, vast amounts of time expended by professional advisers and client on case preparation and the parties' litigation enthusiasm completely sapped.

All too often the effects of litigation and arbitration are:

- polarised positions;
- a drain on the client's managerial time;
- clients who feel out of touch with their own dispute and the victims of a legal *take-over*;
- damaged commercial relationships;
- expensive and long-drawn-out proceedings;
- use of deliberate delaying tactics by a defendant who knows how to play the system;
- a pyrrhic victory for the successful litigant with monies recovered representing a mere fraction of actual expenditure;
- a judgment that is impossible to enforce;
- a belated realisation by the plaintiff that the principal reason for the litigation or arbitration was the impecuniosity of the defendant;
- lawyers who are reluctant to engage in early *reality testing* with their client.

An interesting chart produced by the Academy of Experts demonstrating how parties lose control of their dispute the more formalised the method of dispute resolution adopted is reproduced at Appendix 1. Negotiations allow greatest party control and litigation/arbitration the least.

The perceived failure of litigation and arbitration, first in the United States, where parties are at the mercy of civil juries and the winner will not recover his costs from the losing party, and then in other jurisdictions, has encouraged the growth of ADR. There are three main types of ADR – mediation, conciliation and mini-trial, and various hybrid processes.

Mediation An independent third party, the mediator, assists the parties through individual meetings with them (*caucuses*) as well as joint sessions (a form of *shuttle diplomacy*) to focus on their *real* interests and strengths as opposed to their emotions in an attempt to draw them together towards possible settlement. Crucial to the mediation process is that the independent third party ordinarily does not make recommendations as to what would be an appropriate settlement. He is merely there to assist the parties to find and settle their own agreement. The mediator is quite different from an adjudicator who is called upon to make a decision.

Conciliation A conciliator may be more interventionist than a mediator, and the accompanying process less structured, but he still endeavours to bring disputing parties together and to assist them to focus on the key issues. Conciliation has been well known in the United Kingdom in employment matters for a number of years via ACAS. Given the looseness of ADR terminology the terms *mediator* and *conciliator* are often used interchangeably.

Mini-Trial (Executive Tribunal) Each party presents the issues to senior executives of the disputing parties who are often assisted by a neutral chairman. The parties may be, but not necessarily, represented by lawyers. The chairman, perhaps a lawyer, may advise on the likely outcome of litigation without any binding authority on the parties. After presentation of the issues, the executives try to negotiate a settlement. If successful, the settlement is often set out in a legally enforceable written document. The mini-trial is a misnomer to the extent that it is not really a trial at all. With the legal rules of evidence usually discarded, it is a settlement procedure designed to convert a legal dispute back into a business problem. The mini-trial clearly has a number of advantages:

- a lengthy hearing is eliminated;
- each party's case can be professionally presented but without any formal rules of procedure or evidence;
- those who ultimately decide whether the dispute should be settled (and, if so, on what terms) have the opportunity to be guided by a person with some degree of prestige and outside objectivity;
- the presentations are made to, and the ultimate decision made by, persons with the requisite authority to commit to settlement the bodies which they represent.

Since the late 1980s and early 1990s ADR has been promoted in the United Kingdom by a number of bodies, including the Centre for Dispute Resolution (CEDR), with limited success. ADR remains, for its advocates, an idea whose day has frustratingly not quite arrived. Whether this is the fault of the lawyers or the clients or a combination of the two is unclear. Unlike the psychiatrist's client who may desire change (however difficult that may be) the lawyer's client often retains the lawyer to re-inforce the client's prejudices and to promote a point of view however misguided. Even in the United States, ADR was described in the last two decades as the sleeping giant of American business dispute resolution. Returning to the United Kingdom, in one of the more prominent sectors to use ADR, construction, data suggested ADR is used to resolve 5% of disputes.[17] Brooker and Lavers[18] have concluded "that over 96% of the respondents [in a construction industry survey] have never used any form of ADR. 70% of those respondents who had never used ADR said they would consider doing so, although a surprisingly large proportion (27%) said they did not know ... Only 3% (6 of the 229 respondents) said they would not use ADR". Unlike litigation, the impact of which is somewhat easier to analyse with the availability of national data on the number of referrals to the County Courts and the High Court, the extent to which other methods of dispute resolution have been used is difficult to assess. One problem ADR shares with arbitration is the lack of a single point of organisational control in the United Kingdom. In the same way as arbitrators may be appointed by the Chartered Institute of Arbitrators, the RICS, the RIBA, the ICE or a

---

17 *The Lawyer*, 13th June 1995, at page 15

18 'Perceptions of alternative dispute resolution as constraints upon its use in the UK Construction industry', Construction Management and Economics (1997)15, 519-526 at p.522

number of other appointing bodies, the growth of ADR depends upon the efforts of a number of bodies which at times appear to be in competition with each other rather than merely complementary.

Perhaps the three most prominent promoters of ADR are the Academy of Experts (formerly the British Academy of Experts), CEDR and the lawyer-led ADR Group. What emerges from all such ADR providers is the apparent lack of hard data on the use and growth of ADR in the United Kingdom.

According to its own *Members Handbook* "the British Academy of Experts has been established to promote the better use of Experts, to ensure that the standard of excellence already achieved is maintained and developed and to facilitate the efficient resolution of disputes".[19]

The Academy, which was formed in 1987, has a membership primarily drawn from the ranks of practising expert witnesses. It provides mediation training services to existing and potential third party neutrals. Section 2 of the *Members' Handbook* includes a thumbnail sketch of mediation and how the Academy can assist in setting up mediation hearings. Perhaps most useful are the Academy's *Guidelines for Mediation* under the following headings:

APPOINTMENT OF A MEDIATOR

If the Academy is the appropriate body to oversee the mediation, a short outline of the dispute will be provided to the Academy to assist in the selection of the appropriate neutral. The appointed mediator will require the written acceptance of the parties before beginning the mediation. It is essential that the mediator discloses to the parties any interest he may have in the subject matter of the dispute or connections with any of the parties. The Academy emphasises the need for the mediator to maintain his integrity, to avoid any conduct which may call into question his impartiality and to be aware of any personal factors which might compromise his ability to be or appear fair.

MEETING OF THE PARTIES WITH THE MEDIATOR

Within not more than two weeks of his appointment, the mediator will arrange a meeting of the parties. In addition, he may request, at least seven days before the meeting, that each party provides him with a brief memorandum setting out the relevant facts and issues in dispute and their position on the questions raised. This memorandum will be circulated to the other parties by the mediator. In order to avoid the mediator being deluged with documents, the exchange of information will be controlled by the mediator. Under the Academy's Guidelines the mediator may, with the agreement of the parties, make a site visit or carry out an inspection or seek legal or other technical advice.

CONDUCT OF THE MEETING

The Academy emphasises that the parties should bring to the meeting all documents and information upon which they may wish to rely. The mediator is master of his own procedures:

- he can combine joint and separate sessions with the parties, as he sees fit;
- as the situation demands, he decides which party should make the opening position statement.

Under the Academy's Guidelines the proceedings are neither tape-recorded nor a transcript professionally taken by a stenographer. The parties may appear in person on their own, be assisted by lawyers or work out a flexible approach involving their own advocacy and that of their lawyers. Again, under the Academy's Guidelines, in the absence of agreement being reached, the parties may request the mediator to make a report containing his findings on how the dispute should be settled.

TERMINATION OF THE MEDIATION

As with certain other dispute resolution schemes, a mediator has a discretion to terminate a mediation at any time if he believes that the mediation will not be successful. Similarly, any party to the mediation may withdraw. At the conclusion of the mediation, whether successful or not, the mediator will return to the parties all documents provided to him and destroy any notes that he has taken.

CONFIDENTIALITY

The Academy emphasises the private nature of mediation as a method of dispute resolution. The Academy states that mediation is a *bona fide attempt to resolve disputes between the parties with the entire process consequently being without prejudice*. To protect a mediator's position, anything stated or that emerges or that is disclosed during the mediation is not discoverable or admissible in any subsequent formal proceedings unless the documentation is of a nature which would not ordinarily be subject to legal privilege. To avoid any question of the mediator being called as a witness in later litigation or arbitration, it is stated in bold type:

"No party may call the mediator as a witness in any subsequent legal proceedings to give evidence concerning matters disclosed during mediation."

EXCLUSION OF LIABILITY

Unlike a judge or arbitrator who enjoys immunity from claims that might otherwise be brought as a result of dissatisfaction with the manner in which a court case or arbitration was conducted, a mediator probably (the point has not been litigated in England and Wales) owes a duty of care in negligence to each of the parties as well as a contractual obligation under the contract appointing him to provide his professional services. Therefore, it is essential for a mediator's peace of mind to ensure that all liability is excluded for what he may do or may omit to do during the course of the mediation. This is set out in the Academy's Guidelines, with a further exclusion to the effect that the Academy is not responsible on an agency basis for the conduct of the mediation.

COSTS

As under other similar schemes, the parties are responsible for their own costs and jointly liable for the costs of mediation.

SPECIAL NOTE

Although written in somewhat muted language, which could be stronger, there is an important warning for all those parties who might consider mediation an option for an attempt to resolve their dispute in place of or in addition to conventional litigation or arbitration. If the parties' contract has a well-defined disputes procedure the parties should agree how this is to be modified to accommodate ADR. The Academy also warns that it may be appropriate to take specialist legal advice. The contract may contemplate dispute resolution via the courts or arbitration. If so, a number of issues arise. First, the enthusiasm to use ADR must not lead to a disregard for the possible problems posed by the Limitation Act 1980 and associated legislation. In the case of a contract executed *under hand,* any legal action must be commenced within six years of the breach of contract occurring. If the contract is executed *under seal,* as many construction contracts are, the limitation period is 12 years from the date of the breach of contract. If the claimant's case is based in negligence the limitation period is ordinarily six years from the date of damage occurring, but if the damage is of a hidden (latent) kind and could not ordinarily have been ascertained by the claimant during the primary limitation period of six years, the claimant has, by virtue of the Latent Damage Act 1986, a further three years in which to bring proceedings based on the original negligence, albeit subject to a limitation cut-off date of 15 years from the date when the cause of action originally accrued. Personal injury litigators will also be mindful of the effects of a possibly extended limitation period. It is therefore essential that any party embarking upon a mediation is conscious of problems that may be posed by the expiration of the limitation period. It is one thing to attempt mediation and to be unsuccessful but quite another to embark upon mediation only to find that on its failure there is insufficient time left to pursue the claim through the courts or arbitration.

A number of other considerations may call for lawyer involvement given the flexibility ADR provides:

- Is the mediation simply to end with the parties agreement or failure to agree? If not, is there to be a recommendation from the mediator?
- Following the termination of an unsuccessful mediation session, is there to be a cooling off period before either party may have recourse to the course or arbitration?
- The Academy's mediation summary concludes with a useful Code of Conduct for Mediators:
  - A mediator should not accept an appointment where there is actual, potential or apparent conflict of interest between him and any one of the parties. However, if the parties are aware of the potential conflict, they may endorse his appointment anyway.
  - Mediators cannot work on contingency fees or endorse arrangements whereby the loser pays.
  - A mediator has a duty to comply with the Academy's Guidelines.
  - A mediator must maintain neutrality.
  - A mediator must refuse to act as a witness, advocate or adviser in any subsequent litigation relating to the dispute.
  - Notwithstanding the exclusion of personal liability, the mediator must have suitable professional indemnity insurance.
  - No mediator should publicise his services in a way which could be construed as in bad taste. He should not indulge in inaccurate or misleading publicity.
  - At all times the mediator must comply with the Academy Guidelines and Code of Conduct.

Another prominent ADR provider and the one which appears to have enjoyed the greatest level of press coverage over the last few years or so is the Centre for Dispute Resolution which was formed in 1990, with backing from the Confederation of British Industry. Its basis is somewhat different from the Academy: it has a number of member organisations drawn from commerce and industry as well as support from a large number of City and regional law firms. It has many similarities with the Center for Public Resources in New York. However, like the Academy, CEDR is an important training organisation and appointer of mediators. In addition, to develop the use of mediation in particular market sectors, CEDR has set up specialist Working Groups. The purpose of the Working Groups is to provide a forum in which developments are discussed, initiatives taken and information generally disseminated. CEDR has also been active in providing seminars and presentations in various parts of the United Kingdom, often in conjunction with the Confederation of British Industry, to increase the general level of awareness of ADR amongst businessmen.

CEDR claims to conduct approximately 1–1.5 mediations per week with the value of claims being anywhere between a few thousand pounds and fifty million pounds. Since CEDR was established in 1990 approximately 800 disputes have been referred, although the actual number of disputes resulting in full mediation is unavailable. CEDR has also had experience of mini-trials[20] and Med-Arb[21]. For instance, CEDR was involved in one £200 million mini-trial as special advisers. According to the Academy of Experts the level of activity remains relatively low with the number of referrals being rather in excess of those cases actually resulting in mediation hearings. Perhaps the most positive message is that received from the ADR Group. A spokesman for the Group considered that there had been a considerable change in the public perception of ADR. In 1990 the Group received referrals for mediation at the rate of approximately three per month; of which one, on average, related to the construction industry. At that time only one case would generally proceed as far as a full mediation. Many cases failed to reach a mediation hearing simply because one or other of the participants did not understand ADR, refused to participate or was committed to arbitration or litigation. In the period to 1993 there was a steady growth, with the number of referrals doubling from about three per month to about six per month. The percentage of those

---

20 Chapter 4
21 Chapter 5

relating to the construction industry remained approximately the same. The number of cases which reached a mediation hearing increased from about one-third to about one-half of the cases referred, although the number of construction disputes referred to a hearing did not increase. Apparently the period from mid- 1994 to mid-1995 saw a considerable change, approximately five or six cases referred on average per week. Of those at least 60% actually resulted in a mediation hearing. The success rate achieved in those cases referred to mediation stands at at least 90%. During the period to 1995 there was a corresponding increase in the value of claims referred to mediation. In 1990, for what was then an untried technique, disputes with a value of more than £100,000 were rarely referred. ADR Group is now handling cases across a value range from £50,000 to £2.4 million, with the number of cases at around the £1 million mark becoming more common. It is in multi-party cases that there has been the greatest desire to take cases to mediation, given the high costs of litigation, the complexity of multi-party proceedings and the length of trials which will take several weeks or more. Many modern commercial parties choose not to live with the litigation lottery. A further growth area for mediated settlements has been in professional negligence claims which may involve architects, surveyors or engineers where many insurers impose a requirement upon their lawyers to consider ADR and explain why, if appropriate, it has been rejected. One case handled by ADR Group related to four contractors and an architect in dispute over their liability. Importantly, not one of them alleged that the work carried out on behalf of the client was satisfactory. The mediation was dealt with in two parts. First there was a hearing to establish agreement between the parties as to their degree of liability, and second, a subsequent hearing to mediate between the plaintiff and the contractors and architects in regard to quantum.

Although the Chartered Institute of Arbitrators is primarily concerned with the promulgation of arbitration, nevertheless when ADR began to develop momentum after 1990, the Chartered Institute produced a number of initiatives of its own and is currently considering amendments to its Charter to place the promotion of ADR among its key objectives. However, and although the Chartered Institute's own journal, *Arbitration*, has been instrumental in continuing the debate about the problems of arbitration and the option of ADR, the Chartered Institute has not been seen as a prime promoter of ADR in the United Kingdom.

Despite its patchy record to date, ADR has enjoyed some success in the following fields:

- intellectual property disputes
- partnership disputes
- supply agreements
- private client disputes (*e.g.* trespass and nuisance claims)
- construction industry disputes

The danger remains that ADR may ultimately be categorised by legal historians as an insurrection leading to necessary changes in the litigation *ancien régime* (the impact of Woolf) rather than as a distinctively new method of dispute resolution.

On occasions, litigation has made valiant efforts to put its house in order, *e.g.* the judicial will demonstrated by the *Practice Direction (Civil Litigation: Case Management).*[22]

The impact of the *Practice Direction (Civil Litigation: Case Management)* has let to limited recorded discussion. The powers were used in *Chiltern Street Investments Ltd* (subsequently settled, Current Law 1995 1(1)14, otherwise unreported), the case heard before the Official Referee, His Honour Judge Havery QC. Apparently, after several weeks of evidence, the judge invited the parties to agree reasonable time periods for the presentation of the remaining evidence. The parties, being the plaintiff and two defendants, decided that they would dispense with "blanket" cross-examination with the proviso that a failure to challenge particular evidence would not be determinative but could be a matter for comment by the other parties. Having agreed an overall period for the presentation of evidence, the parties divided that time amongst themselves. In deciding what time to allow to each party, the length of the witness statements was a consideration, as was their content. It was agreed that each party would be limited to a total time to examine and re-examine its own witnesses and a like total to cross-examine another party's witnesses. Although the time for each witness was assessed separately to reach the overall figure, a credit system operated which allowed Counsel to decide how long to take with each witness as the case proceeded. The shorter the time with one witness, the more time freed up for those witnesses who followed. By contrast, at first instance in *John Mowlem & Company v Eagle Star and Others ("Carlton Gate")* the estimate for the cross-examination of 26 witnesses was 90 days. A time limit was imposed of one day's cross-examination for two of the witnesses and one hour each for the remainder.

---

22 [1995] 1 AER 385

Although the *Practice Direction* places greater emphasis on case management, the powers of the courts to avoid prolixity are perhaps more well established than some practitioners might think. In *Banque Keyser Ullmann v Skandia Insurance*, Lord Templeman said:[23]

> "Proceedings in which all or some of the litigants indulge in over-elaboration cause difficulties to judges at all levels in the achievement of a just result. Such proceedings obstruct the hearing of other litigation. A litigant faced with expense and delay on the part of his opponent which threaten to rival the excesses of *Jarndyce v Jarndyce* must perforce compromise or withdraw with a real grievance. In the present case the burdens placed on Steyn J and the Court of Appeal were very great. The problems were complex but the resolution of these problems was not assisted by the length of the hearings or the complexity of the oral evidence and oral argument. The costs must be formidable. I have no doubt that every effort was made in the courts below to alleviate the ordeal but the history of these proceedings is disquieting. The present practice is to allow every litigant unlimited time and unlimited scope so that the litigant and his advisers are able to conduct their case in all respects in the way which seems best to them. The results not infrequently are torrents of words, written and oral, which are oppressive and which the judge must examine in an attempt to eliminate everything which is not relevant, helpful and persuasive. The remedy lies in the judge taking time to read in advance pleadings, documents certified by counsel to be necessary, proofs of witnesses certified by counsel to be necessary, and short skeleton arguments of counsel, and for the judge then, after a short discussion in open court, to limit the time and scope of oral evidence and time and scope of oral argument."

Interestingly, in the *Construction Law Yearbook 1995*[24] the editors refer to two unreported cases. These were the decisions of May J in *Upjohn v Oswald (The Upjohn Company and Another v Oswald; Drucker v Oswald; The Upjohn Company and Another v British Broadcasting Corporation and Another)* and a second case, *Vernon v Bosley*, a decision of Sedley J. The first case was a medical negligence action relating to a drug manufactured by Upjohn called Triazolam. The trial bundles were huge, containing some 36,000 sheets of paper. By careful case management the oral hearing occupied only 62 days. A far longer period of at least one year would have been necessary if a traditional approach had been adopted. The procedure adopted was as follows:

- Written opening submissions with approximately one day for further oral submissions.

---

23 [1991] 2 AC 249, at 280
24 Wiley, p. 199

- Judge's reading time. The judge devoted six days to reading time under the guidance of the parties.
- Evidence in chief was by written witness statements exchanged in advance with a subsequent short period of not more than one hour to allow the witnesses time to become used to the court before being handed over for cross-examination. Any further evidence to be adduced by the parties was the subject of further witness statements.
- Cross-examination. This was by far the longest period of the trial.
- Final submissions. These were written with the parties having a total period of five days divided between them for their presentation.

The second case was a peripatetic action for psychiatric trauma and consequential loss. The action was originally set down for trial in Cardiff with a time estimate of six weeks. By the time the judge went off circuit the evidence had not concluded and the resumed hearing commenced in London. The end of the legal term and certain interlocutory applications to the Court of Appeal meant the judge had not concluded the case before he went on circuit once more to Bristol. As time went on the evidence and the proceedings were seemingly endless. In the words of Sedley J:[25]

> "I hold that in a proper case, which I consider the present one now to be, the Court has the power and, I believe, a duty to achieve finality in its proceedings by placing a fair and realistic limit on the examination, cross-examination and re-examination of the witnesses to be called before it. The limits are not cast in bronze; they may not even be reached, and if they are reached in circumstances in which it is apparent that fairness requires them to be extended, the Court will retain the power to extend them. Such extensions will only be granted where something unforeseen makes it necessary to do so. It is in this way that the Court will retain its overriding discretion to ensure that justice is not impeded by excessive rigidity; but it means that instead of the customary process by which the length of a trial is determined by the length of counsel's examination of witnesses, the time taken in the examination of witnesses becomes a segment of the time allocated for trial in the light of the anticipated needs of the case."

Counsel for the plaintiff and Counsel for the defendant made representations on the judge's power to restrict the timetable. The latter suggested that the judge did not have a power to set time limits.

---

25 Quoted in the *Construction Law Yearbook 1995*, p. 205

Counsel had a fundamental entitlement, within the ordinary bounds of admissibility, to explore issues as Counsel judged best in the client's interests. In addition, Counsel for the defendant suggested that no judge could fetter the evidence to be heard by a prior ruling. A judge had to assess the relevance and admissibility of the evidence which was actually given. However, Sedley J concluded that in the interests of justice it was appropriate to impose a timetable of 26 working hours divided among the five remaining witnesses to cover both their examination-in-chief, cross-examination and re-examination.

The will of the judges now to maintain a strong managerial approach to cases is reflected in the Court of Appeal decision in *Thermawear Ltd* v *Linten and Another*.[26] In the words of the headnote:

> "The Court of Appeal would be most reluctant to interfere with procedural decisions made by a trial judge in the management of the case before him, and will accord him a generous margin of appreciation in the exercise of his discretion in respect of such decisions."

The trial judge, Lightman J, had decided that certain issues be tried in advance of others as preliminary ones. The judge felt that this would render the conduct of the rest of the action more efficient. Apparently the trial judge had referred to the *Practice Direction* and to observations of Lord Roskill and Lord Templeman in *Ashmore* v *Corporation of Lloyd's*.[27]

Although only time would tell whether the trial judge's approach did in fact save time his case management was appropriate and he had not overlooked any relevant factor in making his assessment:

> "In his Lordship's view those observations [*i.e.* the *dicta* in *Ashmore* v *Corporation of Lloyd's*] and that *Practice Direction* were to be read against growing recognition that the luxurious approach to the expenditure of court time was a luxury of the past, indulged in at the expense of litigants as a whole, which could no longer be afforded."

Although perhaps disillusioned with litigation and arbitration, a sea change will be required in the *culture* of most industries before ADR is seen as more than fringe medicine. Perhaps most businesses are not yet ready for principled negotiations and local authorities and other public bodies can hide behind the requirement to satisfy their auditors, a requirement which often produces paralysis and wasted expenditure. Many businesses do not wish to pay or have no money with which to

26 *The Times*, 20th October 1995
27 [1992] 1 WLR 446 at 448 and 453-4

pay. Arbitration or litigation then become equally attractive to both parties locked in dispute. The first party believes he will be able to persuade a court or arbitrator of the legitimacy of his claim by a clever presentation while at the same time the other party views the slow and expensive legal process as a means of denying the first party his legitimate and reasonable financial expectations. The parties may both have entered into a particular contract following a untenable financial analysis. Employees may have an interest in perpetuating litigation or arbitration to conceal their mistakes or over-optimistic assessments from their superiors or even simply to preserve their jobs. However, the position may be changing. Major insurance companies now embrace ADR, civil legal aid will be reformed as some stage to reduce the scope for litigation and Government will not go on increasing the pool of judges. Perhaps most importantly, since the 26th April 1999 the Civil Procedure Rules (the CPR) have been in operation.

The Challenge of ADR

In High Court litigation lawyers cannot now ignore the need at least to pay lip-service to ADR. The most important change prior to implementation of the CPR was the *Practice Direction (Civil Litigation: Case Management)*[28] (reproduced at Appendix 2) which was announced by Lord Taylor of Gosforth, the then Lord Chief Justice, and Sir Richard Scott, the Vice-Chancellor, on 24th January 1995 for use in both the Queen's Bench (including by implication the Official Referee's Court) and Chancery Divisions of the High Court. The message is direct:

> "The paramount importance of reducing the cost and delay of civil litigation makes it necessary for judges sitting at first instance to assert greater control over the preparation for and conduct of hearings than has hitherto been customary."

Important for litigation lawyers is the threat that a failure to conduct cases economically will lead to orders for costs, including a wasted costs order, against such practitioners.

The Practice Direction repeats the earlier *Practice Statement (Commercial Court: Alternative Dispute Resolution)*[29] which

---

28 [1995] 1 WLR 508
29 [1994] 1 WLR 14

recognised the value of ADR. ADR is referred to in the *Practice Direction* under paragraphs 10, 11 and 12:

- Have you or Counsel discussed with your client/clients the possibility of attempting to resolve the dispute by Alternative Dispute Resolution?
- Would some form of Alternative Dispute Resolution resolve or narrow the issues?
- Have you or your client/clients explored with the other parties the possibility of resolving the dispute by Alternative Dispute Resolution?

Where the *Practice Direction* is weak is in not referring to possible sanctions for non-compliance. The cynical solicitor could neuter the application of the ADR provisions either by refusing to discuss them with a client or by always setting the bench mark that his or her cases were ill-suited to ADR. Some lawyers have suggested that an offer by one party to attempt an ADR solution should be set out as a modified Calderbank offer. For instance, the ADR Group proposes the following (also set out in Appendix 3):

"(1) This is formally to advise you that we are offering to mediate in this case.

We make this proposal on the basis that we reserve the right to draw the Court's attention to it on the subject of costs if the dispute proceeds via litigation.

(2) We propose that this matter is one suitable for resolution via a mediation process. We therefore invite you to agree in principle that the matter be resolved via ADR.

We make this proposal on the basis that we reserve the right to draw the Court's attention to it on the subject of costs if the dispute proceeds via litigation."

The above wording is not without its problems. ADR is consensual. How far should a party be penalised for failing to support ADR? Is it unfair pressure nowadays when some insurance company solicitors attempt to get civil legal aid certificates discharged because a plaintiff wants his day in court?

Judicial support for ADR is patchy. Even amongst the specialist construction law judges, the Official Referees, often promoters of change, the support for ADR appears scant. Only the now retired Official Referee, His Honour Judge Fox-Andrews QC, included a direction in his Orders on a Summons for Directions informing the parties of the value of considering resolution of their disputes via one of the ADR techniques.

On 7th June 1996, the Commercial Court under Waller J issued what was, in English terms, a very strongly worded endorsement of ADR in its *Practice Statement (Commercial Cases: Alternative Dispute Resolution)(No 2)*[30] (reproduced at Appendix 4). As the *Practice Statement* indicates:

> "The Judges of the Commercial Court, in conjunction with the Commercial Court Committee, have recently considered whether it is now desirable that any further steps should be taken to encourage the wider use of ADR as a means of settling disputes pending before the Court."

The Commercial Court identified five factors which may encourage the use of ADR. These are:

- a significant reduction in cost;
- a reduction in delays in achieving finality;
- the preservation of existing commercial relationships and market reputation;
- a greater range of settlement solutions than those offered by litigation;
- a substantial contribution to the more efficient use of judicial resources.

However, what is different from any previous judicial comment is the assertion in the *Practice Statement* that judges of the Commercial Court will positively encourage parties to adopt ADR. The *Practice Statement* states:

> "If it should appear to the judge that the action before him or any of the issues arising in it are particularly appropriate for an attempt at settlement by ADR techniques but that the parties have not previously attempted settlement by such means, he may invite the parties to take positive steps to set in motion ADR procedures. The judge may, if he considers it appropriate, adjourn the proceedings then before him for a specified period of time to encourage and enable the parties to take such steps. He may, for this purpose, extend the time for compliance by the parties, or either of them, with any requirement of the Rules of the Supreme Court, or previous interlocutory orders in the proceedings."

A further radical departure in the *Practice Statement* is the endorsement of the principle of *early neutral evaluation*. This is a recognition that judges, particularly under the English adversarial system, have to listen to considerable amounts of evidence which ordinarily it is the parties' right to lead, even if the judge is privately of

---

the opinion that much of the evidence will not greatly assist him in coming to an appropriate conclusion. By permitting early neutral evaluation, perhaps allowing the judge to express a view at an interlocutory stage on close of pleadings, lengthy trials may be curtailed. Under the *Practice Statement*, the assigned judge of the Commercial Court may provide the evaluation, or arrange for another judge to do so. Of course, the judge cannot impose early neutral evaluation upon the parties unless the parties otherwise agree. If there is early neutral evaluation which does not result in settlement, the particular judge will not take any further part in the proceedings.

Where the *Practice Statement* is also tougher is the wide discretion given to judges assessing costs. The judge may consider that ADR has been deployed. The parties must report back to the judge if ADR is attempted and fails, although, quite properly, the substantive contact between the parties and their advisors is not to be made known to the judge.

There are certain other ADR initiatives. ADR has been tried out to a limited extent in the County Court[31]. From May 1996 the Central London County Court operated a one-year pilot scheme to allow mediation of certain civil disputes. The scheme applied to disputes in the £3000 – £10000 range. Parties who opted for mediation did so without prejudice to their court-based rights. They had the benefit of a three-hour session with a trained mediator from one of the ADR providers outside court hours between 4.30 p.m – 7.30 p.m. Each side paid £25 towards the mediator's costs with the mediation arranged within 28 days. A similar, two-year scheme operated in the Patents County Court in London. In addition, the Patents County Court is offering arbitration by a technical arbitrator included in a court list. Also, the Lord Chancellor's Department[32] has produced a useful booklet on resolving disputes by methods other than litigation and implicitly endorsed ADR. ADR has now spread to medical negligence under Practice Direction 49, where from 1st November 1996, Master Foster has been assigned to hear all interlocutory applications in the Queen's Bench Division relating to medical negligence claims. Now, at the first hearing of the summons for directions, each party must state whether ADR has been considered, if not why not, and if ADR has been rejected, why. This development is crucial with the legal aid fund being dedicated in huge amounts to the pursuit of medical negligence cases. The text of Practice Direction 49 is found at Appendix 5.

---

31 *The Times*, 27th August 1996, Frances Gibb
32 *Resolving Disputes Without Going to Court*, Lord Chancellor's Department, December 1995

Under the CPR, ADR plays a much more prominent role. According to Rule 1.4(2)(e) active case management includes:

> "Encouraging the parties to use an alternative dispute resolution procedure if the court considers that appropriate and facilitating the use of such procedure."

This all ties in with the CPR being subject to Part 1, Rule 1.1(1) to the overriding objective requiring the courts to "deal with cases justly". ADR is expressly provided for in Part 26, Rule 26.4. Under Rule 26.4(1):

> "A party may, when filing the completed allocation questionnaire, make a written request for the proceedings to be stayed while the parties try to settle the case by alternative dispute resolution or other means."

Perhaps more controversially, under Rule 26.4(2):

> "Where –
> (a) all parties request a stay under paragraph (1); or
> (b) the court, of its own initiative, considers that such a stay would be appropriate,
> the court will direct that the proceedings be stayed for one month."

The court may extend the stay "until such date or for such specified period as it considers appropriate" (Rule 26.4(3)).

If parties do not follow ADR, the question arises what sanctions there may be. There are new costs' provisions in the CPR. Under Rule 44.5(3), the court must have regard, when assessing the amount of costs, to a number of factors including:

> "(a) the conduct of all the parties, including in particular –
> (i) conduct before, as well as during, the proceedings; and
> (ii) the effort made, if any, before and during the proceedings in order to try to resolve the dispute."

Obviously, at the time of writing, the CPR are new and time will tell how well they are developed and deployed by the courts. Judges may be reluctant to stay cases to ADR, conscious of the impression which affects selection criteria. In addition, judges may conclude ADR works against the interests of the participants to a dispute where, for instance, the amount claimed falls within the County Court small claims limit and County Court arbitration is more cost effective than relatively expensive ADR. In addition, on occasions, a claimant will know a defendant is procrastinating and, under the fast track, rapid progress to trial is more attractive.

Chapter 2

Using Mediation to Resolve Disputes

Practical Concerns

Many clients seem to go to their solicitors' offices in the belief that litigation can resolve all their problems. However, such clients have not made a realistic assessment of their own position. They know what they would like their case to be and what form the facts should take but are often reluctant to look at the reality presented by the facts. In this they are frequently assisted by their lawyers. Most lawyers wish to be helpful and to highlight the positive features in their clients' cases. That said, it is a bad lawyer who at the same time does not address the client's mind to the weaker or more problematic elements. Those lawyers who do identify weak points are accused of being negative and may be subjected to intense bullying from a client who wishes his lawyer to stand shoulder to shoulder with him without undue dissent. It is easy to adopt the response, whenever a dispute arises, issue a Writ and see what happens.[1] Such an approach is often supported by the simplistic statement that *most cases settle.* Indeed, most cases (well in excess of 80%) do settle at some stage prior to trial but many of those settle only when high legal costs have already been incurred and the scope for creative negotiations has been lessened. By the time settlement is seriously talked about, the substantial fees incurred to lawyers and expert witnesses have become real bones of contention and ones which are accommodated by each of the parties deciding to bear his own costs.

People do win legal trials but more often than not after a long and bloody battle; conversely legal trials do produce heavy losers. To litigate is to play a lottery: ultimately each party has to possess the

---

1 A notable example of litigation which backfired was Mowlem's Carlton Gate claim. According to *Contract Journal*, 10th August 1995: "What is amazing is that Mowlem continued its battle even after declaring a £123 million loss for 1993. On what quality of legal advice? Some might ask. One lawyer speculated: 'You always try to give the client some good news in the early days. Perhaps that's what ... did, and a bandwagon was set up'."

capacity to lose. Frequently the use of litigation is justified by stating that the opposing party is wholly unreasonable, someone with whom you cannot negotiate and in any event the prosecution of the claim is a matter of *principle*. The experienced lawyer advises his clients – never litigate principles, only law. Litigation does have a serious role to play where there are clear legal questions in issue, particularly if they favour one party, but if the dispute is centred on fact, and fact alone, litigation is not the best medium for the resolution of a dispute. Yet, as the primary advisers in any dispute are the lawyers, it needs an experienced, or sufficiently altruistic, lawyer to state that a particular dispute requires a technical assessment or an independently brokered settlement rather than risk becoming a playground for legal sophistry.

The way lawyers are trained in the United Kingdom has tended to separate dispute resolution from any associated sociological, moral or religious concerns and to reduce dispute resolution to a purely legal exercise. Certain religious and ethnic groups may have a cultural bias in favour of particular methods of dispute resolution. It has been suggested[2] that the Beth Din (Court of the Chief Rabbi) which fulfils the functions of, *inter alia*, dispute arbitration and mediation is now, on occasions, being asked to mediate in disputes involving non-Jews. In addition, in other cultures, for example the Asia/Pacific Rim, there may be a cultural preference in favour of mediation as opposed to adjudicative methods of dispute resolution:

> "In various Asian Countries, there is a profound societal philosophical preference for agreed-upon solutions. Rather than a cultural bias towards 'equality' in relationships, there exists an intellectual and social predisposition towards a natural hierarchy which governs conduct in interpersonal relations. Asian cultures frequently seek a 'harmonious' solution, one which tends to preserve the relationship, rather than one which, while arguably, factually and legally 'correct' may severely damage the relationship of the parties involved".[3]

Donahey identified the Chinese approach as being in keeping with traditional Confucianism:[4]

> "Within traditional Confucianism, going back thousands of years, there is a concept known as *li* which concerns the social norms of behavior within the five natural status relationships: emperor and subject, father and son, husband and wife, brother and brother, or friend and friend.

---

2 Research data collated by the writer
3 'Seeking Harmony', M. Scott Donahey, (1995) 61 *JCI Arb* 4, p. 279
4 *ibid.*, p. 280

Li is intended to be persuasive, not compulsive and legalistic, a concept which governs good conduct and is above legal concepts in societal importance. The governing legal concept, *fa* is compulsive and punitive. While having the advantage of legal enforceability, *fa* is traditionally below *li* in importance. The Chinese have always considered the resort to litigation as the last step, signifying that the relationship between the disputing parties can no longer be harmonized. Resort to litigation results in loss of face, and discussion and compromise are always to be preferred. Over time the concept of *fa* and *li* have become confused and the concept of maintaining the relationship and, therefore, face, has become part of the Chinese legal system."

Donahey highlights a similar position exists under the other Asian legal systems, including the Korean one.

Traditionally, those who could not resolve their disputes amicably by way of a sensible settlement were automatically propelled towards litigation. A potential litigant, offered a bad settlement, might have felt the poignancy of Hamlet's soliloquy:

"Whether 'tis nobler in the mind to suffer the slings and arrows of outrageous fortune, or to take arms against a sea of troubles, and by opposing end them?"[5]

or be put in mind of Proverbs[6]

"Starting a quarrel is like breaching a dam;
so drop the matter before a dispute breaks out"

Mediation offers the middle way between the unpredictability of litigation and simply giving into a bad settlement in those situations where mediation is a suitable option; but to gain support ADR must offer two way benefits. Apart from the general ADR providers, such as CEDR and the Academy of Experts, which fulfil in part a proselytising role, particular industries have developed their own mediation procedures. For intellectual property disputes there are the WIPO Mediation Rules effective from 1st October 1994 which are reproduced at Appendix 6. Although produced to service the world intellectual property market they are readily transferable to other disputes.

In assessing whether or not a case is appropriate for mediation, the following factors may assist a party in making a decision whether to litigation or mediate:

---

5 *Hamlet*, William Shakespeare, Act III, Sc. 1, l. 57-60
6 Chap. 17, v. 14

- The parties have and want to maintain a commercial relationship.
- Both parties have a mutual interest in a quick resolution of the dispute.
- Both parties recognise that litigation will provide an unacceptable drain on their managerial time, be expensive, long drawn out and unpredictable.
- Neither party wishes to have the publicity that litigation may bring them.
- The parties have come to understand that mediation may provide them with the best option to have their day in court, a form of catharsis, yet carried out in the most cost-effective way possible.
- The parties have already experienced litigation and mediation in other disputes and have learnt the value of mediation and the *downside* of litigation.
- There may be problems with witness availability or quality and the full intensity of a possible trial is best avoided.

Mediation may *not* work:

- Where the dispute is centred more on law than on fact and established precedent strongly favours one party over the other. In those circumstances litigation, including summary judgment under RSC Order 14 or 14A, is more appropriate.
- One party wishes to delay the resolution of the dispute for as long as possible. If the dispute is based on a contract, the parties must be mindful of the limitation period. Under *simple* contracts, the limitation period operates for six years from the date of the contract breach occurring. If the contract is *under seal* the limitation period is 12 years. It would not be advantageous to commence a mediation just about the time when the limitation period was running out.
- Either one or other, or even both, the parties are not acting in good faith, are happy to exaggerate or even lie to a mediator and have no real commitment to resolve the dispute.
- One or other of the parties believes that litigation will be a complete vindication of his position.
- There is inequality of bargaining position between the parties. This does not necessarily manifest itself in their respective sizes, although this may often be a crucial factor. Conceivably, a small sub-contractor could mediate a dispute with a large main contractor if the business affairs of each

created a close dependency and if, for instance, at the time of the mediation the sub-contractor could rely upon an enhanced position because of his importance to the main contractor on other projects.

- Where the position of one of the parties is strongly influenced by a particular individual in the organisation who has a position to protect, has perhaps made a mistake and is unwilling to recognise the error and can wrongly use his rank within the organisation to maintain inappropriate litigation.

- Where one or other of the parties has developed a *culture* of late or non payment.

- Where one or other of the parties either lacks the resources or the money to face his responsibilities under a particular contract and is insufficiently mature to be open and is happy to manipulate litigation to conceal his own weaknesses.

- Where one or other of the parties is answerable to the district auditors, in the case of a public authority, or, if an insurance-backed client, the perceptions of the professional indemnity insurers need to be satisfied. The chant frequently arises that in the absence of a *negotiated settlement* public auditors and insurers require a *litigated* solution. Mediation has about it the whiff of *horse-trading*, whereas public auditors and insurers are looking to establish rights and obligations (the simple quest for right and wrong) and are not seeking a commercial deal. What however such people choose to forget is that most disputes, even if litigated, do result ultimately in a deal being struck which is often lacking in finesse and owes nothing to pre-existing contractual rights and obligations. Clearly, the present attitude of insurers will need to alter radically and publicly to provide further momentum to the growth of ADR in the United Kingdom where many defences are essentially run by insurers. To be fair, many insurers are now more conscious of ADR and are pushing their solicitors into its endorsement.

- The dispute is one where the creation of precedent is desirable, as, for instance, in the case of class actions in personal injury claims or where questions of public or administrative law are in issue on judicial review applications.

- The disclosure of confidential information, albeit on a without-prejudice basis, and a failed attempt at ADR may put a party at a psychological disadvantage in subsequent litigation or arbitration proceedings as well as raise complex questions of legal professional privilege.

How can a party commence a mediation? The process is not necessarily as simple as issuing a writ because it requires the agreement of both parties to the use of mediation. Where lawyers have been instructed and they are lukewarm about ADR they may actively dissuade a client from considering the option. ADR is more likely to occur where both parties have lawyers committed to ADR or one or other of the parties (but preferably both) have seen the advantages of ADR in a previous dispute. Mediation is possible in three situations:

- By a contract clause which precludes the use of litigation until the ADR route has been properly explored. Admittedly the enforceability of ADR clauses is questionable if one of the parties decides to litigate but at least the party advocating ADR can point to the contract to support his stance.
- Even if there is no mediation clause in the contract, the parties may agree, on the occurrence of the dispute, that the particular dispute will be referred to mediation rather than to arbitration or litigation in the courts. Here, a claimant may be reluctant to suggest ADR. Does it send out the wrong message, *i.e.* the claimant has doubts about the strength of his own case? How does he win over the cynical opponent who taunts him with the 'real men litigate' innuendo? Such a problem may not disappear rapidly. Generally greater training in conflict management in universities and other colleges is necessary together with more acceptance that mistakes do occur from time to time and are part of the human condition.
- Litigation or arbitration may already have been commenced and the parties subsequently decide that they wish to try to resolve their differences by mediation. A useful time at which to consider the suitability of mediation is at close of pleadings. This will be when the parties have exchanged Statement of Claim, Defence and Counterclaim (if any), the Reply to the Defence and the Defence to Counterclaim (if any) and completed the task of exchanging and answering Requests for Further and Better Particulars of any pleading. It may not be too late to consider the use of ADR even once discovery and inspection have occurred but before incurring the heavy expense of final proofing of witnesses, preparing

for and conducting any trial. It is harder to sell ADR at this late stage given that the vast majority of cases do implode and clients resent what they see as a further layer of cost.

Model ADR contract clauses prepared by CEDR are re-produced with the kind permission of CEDR in Appendix 7. The best option for selling ADR is to include ADR in contracts as a principal obligation if things go wrong and disputes need to be resolved.

Although parties may choose their own *bespoke* mediation procedure, either the contract clause may define the procedures to be adopted or refer to a standard mediation procedure of the type found, for instance, in the 1990 Chartered Institute of Arbitrators *Guidelines for Conciliation and Mediation* (reproduced at Appendix 8) or the CEDR Model Mediation Procedure, the latter being reproduced in Appendix 9. There is much to be said for the contract defining the mediation procedure. Once a dispute arises time will be lost if a procedure needs to be agreed and unnecessary rancour could set in.

Although ADR, including mediation, appears to have much to commend it as far as clients are concerned, the cry may go up in certain quarters – so what's in it for the lawyers? Many people outside the law do not accept that lawyers have necessarily taken to heart the Bible demand:

> "Blessed are the peace-makers: for they shall be called the children of God"[7]

Law is, however, as was stated in Chapter 1, a consumer service and the greater the client's awareness of the range of procedures open to their lawyers, the greater the pressure will be from the informed client to produce remedies which are suited to the client's true needs. Busy commercial men should crave solutions rather than sterile and expensive legal battles. Therefore, litigation lawyers cannot ignore the growth of ADR and its potential attractiveness to a business community that, in the absence of insurance, often cannot afford litigation.

If lawyers are prepared to view mediation positively, it provides them with the following opportunities. It may over time change the nature of their workload but not leave them with a depleted file load and falling fee income.

---

7 *Matthew*, Chap. 5, v. 9

- They can advise their clients on one of the important factors in the dispute, namely the client's legal rights.
- They can advise their clients in the choice of a suitable dispute resolution procedure.
- They can assist clients in the preparation of cases for ADR.
- They can represent clients during mediation meetings and mini-trials (the latter being discussed in Chapter 3).
- They can assist clients to prepare and complete appropriate settlement agreements which are legally enforceable.
- They can assist clients to set up contracts which contain more imaginative dispute resolution clauses than the tired formulae that all disputes will be resolved by litigation in the High Court or through arbitration.

Lawyers can also assist with the following:

- Which ADR technique is most suited to the dispute in question.
- Any time limits to be imposed (if none are set in a contractual clause) for the completion of the reference to ADR.
- In the absence of prior agreement, how the mediator should be chosen; should he have particular qualifications?
- What documentation should be prepared and possibly exchanged prior to the mediation sessions.
- Should the mediator be able to make recommendations, either of a non-binding or binding nature in the absence of settlement?
- Should the mediator provide a written report setting out his recommendations if the mediation fails?
- An analysis of what the disputant's objectives and interests are from resolution of the dispute.
- An analysis of the legal issues, separating them from the factual ones.
- Deciding the method of presentation to be adopted before the mediator – should the lead presenter be technically or legally qualified?
- Analysing whether the dispute has crystallised to a sufficient degree and the other party's papers been sufficiently disclosed to make a sensible assessment of the value of ADR possible?
- Is it a matter in which the client's professional indemnity insurers are likely to be interested – thereby making notification to them essential?

- A risk assessment of the likely outcome if the matter were to be pursued via litigation or arbitration.
- Are there any general policy considerations, or the requirement for legal precedent, which render litigation in the High Court more advantageous to the client?
- If the dispute were to be litigated or arbitrated in the traditional way, is either party likely to have witness problems – witnesses who are now working overseas or for other employers; witnesses who may be hostile to a former employer; witnesses whose co-operation will be expensive to buy; witnesses whose performance in court is likely to be poor?
- Are the documents in such a mess or lacking in completeness as to render recourse to litigation or arbitration undesirable?

The use of ADR, rather than litigation or arbitration, is not an excuse for poor case preparation even if the more rapid pace of ADR may lead to more limited (albeit still thorough) preparation than would a full trial. To present a case effectively at a mediation session, to discuss appropriate settlement figures or, as the case may be, *trade-offs*, all require a full understanding of the issues arising out of the dispute both by the outside advisers and the party's own senior personnel. For the lawyers it is essential to:

- Confirm that all necessary information is available for the mediation sessions.
- Know the facts of the dispute thoroughly from both perspectives, take necessary witness statements to be incorporated into a position paper, collate these and understand them thoroughly.
- Identify and analyse the important or likely to be contested legal issues.
- Complete a risk analysis chart of the strengths and weaknesses of the client's case and, as far as possible, the strengths and weaknesses of the other side's case.
- Determine who should attend the mediation sessions on behalf of the client, ensuring that those who do attend have sufficient authority and are of sufficient standing within the organisation to reach binding agreements, make concessions and engage in necessary trade-offs.
- Determine, in conjunction with the client's representatives, the best and worst positions on liability and, as far as possible, quantum – giving due regard to those issues in the

opponent's case which may objectively cause a change of opinion.

- Develop a negotiation plan which accommodates the offer or demand that the client would ultimately be happy to settle for following the mediation sessions.
- Decide, prior to the mediation sessions, if there are any facts that are not to be disclosed to the other party so as to be prepared to inform the mediator immediately about them in strict confidence.
- Be aware that there is no value in simply holding on to information for the sake of it, adopting the litigator's favoured stance of keeping your powder dry.
- Consider with the client whether the opening address in joint sessions with the mediator and the other party will be made by the client or by the lawyers.
- Produce an analysis of the likely costs pattern if the dispute were to be resolved by litigation or arbitration, including provision for expert witness and counsel's fees.
- Assess whether there is any value in proceeding via litigation to create a precedent or because important points of contract interpretation arise or issues of public or administrative law need to be resolved.
- Even if judgment is achievable through litigation, assess how far that judgment is recoverable.
- Assess what is the hidden cost to the client in having key personnel tied up in the preparations for trial, potentially for many months.
- Assess whether there are any tax advantages that may be available to either party if a dispute is resolved quicker through mediation at a particular time rather than years hence through the courts or arbitration.
- Consider what information is to be volunteered to the mediator and the order of its disclosure together with what information is to be retained from both mediator and opponent.

Presentation of any case at an ADR session (and the prior preparation) requires organisational skills and an awareness of what a party wishes to achieve as well as an understanding of what mediation is. The approach has much in common with principled negotiations as popularised by Roger Fisher and William Ury.[8] The

---

8 *Getting to Yes – Negotiating Agreements Without Giving In*, Business Books Limited, 1991

use of principled negotiations involves deciding issues on the merits by some objective standard rather than by resort to positional bargaining. The latter approach encourages each side to take a position and stubbornly hold to it rather than focus on their underlying concerns and needs. There are four fundamentals for principled negotiations:

- *People*: Separate the people from the problem
- *Interests:* Focus on interests, not positions
- *Options*: Generate a variety of possibilities before deciding what to do
- *Criteria:* Insist that the result be based on some objective standard

There are two basic approaches to mediation. These are the *facilitative approach* and the *evaluative approach*. ADR based on principled negotiations, *i.e.* mediation in its purest form aided by a third party neutral, is the facilitative approach. The mediator is a catalyst, assisting the parties to explore their own positions and that of the other party, looking for solutions based on their common interests. Ordinarily, the mediator would not express an opinion or propose a settlement in this form of ADR. Some forms of ADR promote an evaluative or rights-based approach. Here, the mediator evaluates the strengths and weaknesses of each party's case and makes recommendations. His purpose is to coax the parties towards a more realistic position so that the dispute may be resolved. A notable example of this technique is found in the civil engineering industry, where under the ICE Conciliation Procedure (1994) the conciliator makes a recommendation to the parties if agreement is not achieved following joint sessions and separate caucus sessions. A recommendation may become binding after a prescribed cooling off period. The ICE Procedure is reproduced at Appendix 10. It is a first rate scheme for the resolution of many disputes, not merely those relating to civil engineering and is an answer to those critics of mediation who fear an expensive talking shop and no resolution of a dispute. American commentators have agonised long and hard over the use of a co-ercive or adjudicative element in mediation. According to two such writers:

"Under both the facilitative and evaluative approaches the mediator may be interventionist although the nature of his intervention will differ. If acting as a facilitator, the mediator may provide ideas to free the parties from an apparent impasse, looking to identify for them their interests. Whenever a facilitative mediator offers solutions this must be done so as not to alienate the parties, leaving them to adopt ideas as their own and in their own time. As an evaluator, the mediator can be rather less coy in getting his views across and may work aggressively towards getting the parties to accept his recommendation.

One of the great values of mediation is to promote a realistic understanding by each party of the other's interests. ...

What is evaluation? It is a process in which a neutral expresses an opinion as to the likely outcome or value of a legal claim or defense were it to be adjudicated. Evaluation can focus on either a single issue or on the overall result in a case. It can be expressed in ranges ("the damages could range from $25,000 to $75,000"), numeric probabilities ("40% chance"), or as a precise number ("a $100,000 case"). An evaluation can be expressed with certainty ("The plaintiff will win...") or studied vagueness ("I have some doubts about...").

Evaluation is sometimes hard to distinguish from "reality testing". Almost all mediators are willing to reality test – that is, to question disputants about the strengths and weaknesses of their cases. In this role, a mediator acts as a devil's advocate, pushing the disputants to become more realistic without completely revealing his or her personal opinion about the merits.

Mediators may be less successful than they think at hiding their opinions about the merits. Reality testing is a spectrum in which the line between mere testing and evaluation is not always clear. For example, a phrase such as "What are your thoughts on the causation issue?" is unlikely to be controversial. But such commonly asked questions as "Do you think there's a problem on causation?"; How would you answer this argument on causation?"; "Don't you have a real causation problem here?"; or "You don't think that's an issue?" are increasingly likely to be interpreted as evaluative opinions. Even if the language used by a mediator is scrupulously neutral, his or her feelings about the strength of an argument may well show unconsciously in facial expressions and body language. It is likely that litigants perceive evaluation going on in many situations where a mediator would describe his or her behavior as "reality testing."[9]

A good mediator, whether facilitative or evaluative, should put the parties at their ease, not overtly take sides and be able to encourage the parties to consider issues rather than dwell on personalities. Above all, he must be of independent spirit and not linked to either of the parties. It is desirable that at the mediation sessions a co-operative negotiating strategy with neutrality of language and

---

9 "*Using Evaluations in Mediation*", Dwight Golann and Marjorie Gorman Aaron, *Dispute Resolution Journal*, Spring 1997, pp. 8-9

demeanour (but not such as to signal indifference) is adopted rather than an aggressive or hectoring tone. First, and this is to be distinguished from weak bargaining, the common ground and shared values are to be identified and confirmed. This strikes a positive note, may immediately reduce the areas in dispute and provides each of the parties with a feeling that the process is beneficial as they recognise the common ground. Some people suggest that experience of the customs and practice of the industry in which the dispute occurs is useful but not essential in a mediator. An ideal mediator should have the following virtues:

Empathy The ability to get on with the parties, understand their positions, even if he does not agree with them or sees that they are wrong, and the ability to deflect the parties from what may be their tenaciously held views gently and without causing them irritation. Any change of position must be genuinely the party's own shift, so that there are no feelings of having been bullied. The mediator must be seen to be a good listener.

Patience The ability to wait for the parties to shift their position in their own time when perhaps the mediator believes that they could have come to obvious conclusions far quicker than they achieve in practice.

Self-assurance and clarity of thought Being able to instil a sense of confidence in the minds of the parties, with a game plan for what is to be achieved, without hectoring or obviously leading the parties. A good mediator will ask questions which are intelligent and provoke answers, rather than make speeches.

Ingenuity The capacity to bring in new ideas when the discussions appear to be flagging or on the point of failing, including the power to think laterally and to propose novel solutions for the parties to adopt and promote as their own ideas.

Stamina An ability to keep going and maintain concentration. The mediation sessions may take place over an extended period of time, and although there may be scope for breaks during the early sessions, as momentum increases towards possible agreement, subsequent sessions may occupy fairly considerable periods before there is room for a natural break to occur.

There are subtle distinctions between the facilitative and evaluative approaches. In the former, with negotiating skills dominating, it is not essential to be an expert in the area of the dispute. Although specific expertise in the subject matter of the dispute can be useful to seek solutions, it can lead the mediator to the adoption of positions. An evaluative mediator must have sufficient technical knowledge to make an evaluation and will be more assertive.

Unlike litigation and arbitration, mediation has no rule book, although ADR organisations such as CEDR have some standard procedures. So how does a mediation progress? Before the formal mediation sessions commence the problem of the seating arrangements for the parties needs to be addressed.[10] The opposing camps must not be seated in such a way as to create in their minds the feeling that a particular party is being especially advantaged. Ideally the representatives of the various parties should be equidistant from the mediator at the opening session so that eye contact can be engaged with any necessary person. For that reason a round table is probably best avoided. Depending on the number of parties either a rectangular or an 'H' configuration is better. Both arrangements place the parties' representatives at equidistance from the mediator, thereby allowing him to engage either side in dialogue or listen to a point without antagonising the other.

If position papers are submitted to the mediator, they should be shorter rather than longer. A good model to adopt is the principle in the Case Management Practice Direction of the High Court which requires skeleton arguments not to exceed 20 pages of double-spaced A4 typescript or work to an agreed word limit of perhaps 5,000 words. Although the precise format of position papers will depend upon the nature of the dispute they might include the following:

- Introductory remarks and a positive indication that it is the client's wish to work towards settlement.
- A resumé of the facts of the case as seen by the client but highlighting any agreements or disagreements that are believed to exist in regard to the particular facts.
- An analysis of liability and quantum.

---

10 In exceptional circumstances there may be a conference-call mediation: a landlord and tenant dispute where the parties were in Texas and San Mateo, California, respectively was subject to mediation by telephone: *Consensus*, April 1996, No. 30, p. 9, MAT-Harvard Public Disputes Program.

In preparing for and making the subsequent opening oral submissions it is essential for those involved to be realistic and honest although no party will be instantly open, revealing all the unfavourable parts of his case. Like any other negotiation he will filter information. As with the position papers, the oral submissions should have a time limit imposed upon them, avoid specific settlement figures, not emphasise what are considered to be deal breakers and at all costs avoid emotive language. It would be futile to commence any mediation session with the statement "I'll settle for £50,000 and not a penny less". The other party will simply spend the rest of the period taken to deliver the opening statement thinking up all the reasons possible why there is no entitlement to £50,000, rather than listen to the facts of the case as the party presenting his case perceives them.

In his handling of the mediation sessions, the mediator must remain aware throughout that the parties do not wish to be cajoled or coaxed into a compromise settlement and that mediation is not simply about splitting the difference. It is all about trying to achieve win win solutions (*i.e.* ones both parties can tolerate even if without the feeling of being a clear winner), unless the emphasis is on an evaluation being achieved.

Once opening presentations have been made, the mediator will discuss the issues raised to clarify the key points in his own mind and even pose the question to each of those present – 'What do you want?' This may be done initially with both parties present, subsequently holding individual meetings with the parties and their representatives. In the private or caucus sessions which follow the joint opening session, the mediator will discuss in confidence the strengths and weaknesses of the parties' respective cases and get them to focus on what is in their best interests. He may propose possible solutions which may be either his idea or suggested by the other party.

Once the divisions between the parties appear to be narrowing or disappearing the mediator may well attempt further joint sessions to close any remaining gap with a view to the parties achieving a clear and enforceable settlement. If the mediator has an evaluative role he can make recommendations (if an impasse is reached) for the settlement of the dispute. In any mediation the caucus sessions are essential. They permit mediators to develop a clear understanding of the respective cases, private agendas and possible settlement positions, without the parties disclosing to the other their true wants and weaknesses in a manner which would undermine any momentum towards settlement. Mediators will, however, be realists and appreciate that even in the private sessions not everything is revealed to them.

There is no set period to allocate to a particular mediation to achieve success although the law of diminishing returns may well set in after two-three days. However mediation can be carried out on an intermittent basis over several weeks or, although unsuccessful, predispose the parties to agreeing their settlement later once the mediator has departed the scene. Mediation is a constant process of trying to respond to the parties' personal requirements while, at the same time, deflating their adherence to positions that cannot be justifiably held. Two illustrative examples of how mediation can work are set out below.

Mr and Mrs X and Mr and Mrs Y were owners of adjoining properties. There was a large bushy hedge marking the boundary at the rear of both properties. Mr and Mrs X went on holiday only to find on their return that the hedge had been removed by Mr and Mrs Y and a fence erected. Mr and Mrs X asked Mr and Mrs Y to remove the fence which they failed to do. Mr and Mrs X went to their solicitors who informed Mr and Mrs Y by letter before action that if the fence were not removed to the actual line of the boundary within seven days legal proceedings would commence in the County Court. The fence remained where it was and the proceedings started. Damages and/or an injunction and a declaration as to the line of the boundary was sought. Those proceedings limped on for six years until mediation was recommended. During the process of the mediation Mr and Mrs X were seen by the mediator. He asked them what they wished to achieve. Mrs X said this was obvious. They wanted an apology! The mediation was satisfactorily resolved in 30 minutes.

The need to recognise the *hidden agenda* of a particular party emerges from the following.

A roofer sustained terrible injuries when he fell into the well of a building. Liability was not an issue from the defendant's solicitors/insurers and the only arguments related to quantum of damage. The plaintiff argued that he required £200,000 specially to adapt his home to meet his requirements. The insurance company was not prepared to offer more than £100,000. Instead of legal proceedings mediation was used during which it transpired that, for *policy* reasons, the insurers could not offer £200,000 under this particular head of claim. However, the insurers were happy to provide the plaintiff with a further £100,000 on the basis that it was spread across other heads of claim and thereby lost.

In dispute resolution the terms mediation and conciliation are often used interchangeably while other commentators and ADR providers attempt to differentiate between the two. The Academy of Experts makes no distinction between conciliation and mediation, whereas CEDR and the Chartered Institute of Arbitrators distinguish conciliation from mediation. CEDR categorises conciliation as an informal attempt to bring parties together to resolve a dispute. This may subsequently lead to mediation or another suitable means of settlement. Mediation is more formalised. According to the Chartered Institute of Arbitrators, conciliation is:

> "... a process whereby a conciliator investigates the facts of the case, attempts to reconcile the opposing contentions of the parties and prompts them to formulate their own proposals for settlement of the case by indicating the strong and weak points of their arguments and the possible consequences of failure to settle. The conciliator will not usually make a recommendation of his/her own for settlement of the dispute, however, he/she acts as a catalyst for settlement by the parties themselves."

A number of well respected and developed dispute resolution methods describe themselves as conciliation procedures. Under one – the civil engineering industry's Conciliation Procedure 1994 (Appendix 10) – the conciliator is expressly empowered, in the absence of a facilitated solution, to recommend to the parties how the dispute should be settled. Civil engineering contracts state that if arbitration is not then commenced within a prescribed period, the recommendation becomes final and binding.

The ICE (Institution of Civil Engineers) Conciliation Procedure, first devised for use with the ICE Conditions of Contract for Minor Works 1988, now serves, in its 1994 revision, the ICE Conditions of Contract 6th Edition, the ICE Design & Construct Conditions of Contract and the ICE Conditions of Contract for Minor Works. Although much criticised, the ICE Design and Construct Conditions 1992 originally provided for mandatory conciliation. With mandatory conciliation seen by many as self-contradictory, at the time of writing, the ICE is proposing the removal of mandatory conciliation from the Design and Construct Conditions.

Turning to the mechanics of the Conciliation Procedure, this is set out in three sections. First, there is a general Preface which explains the main differences between conciliation and arbitration. Second, the Conciliation Rules are set out in 23 numbered paragraphs with the third part of the Conciliation Procedure booklet being a Conciliator's Agreement, together with a Schedule in which details of fees can be set out. The Rules seek to achieve maximum clarity with the minimum of technical legal language. In this aim they are very largely successful.

The aims of the panel when drafting the Conciliation Procedure (1994) were to emphasise:

- achieving a settlement;
- the non-binding nature of the process;
- the confidential nature of the process;
- the process is *without prejudice* and anything said or conceded will not affect the parties' positions if a settlement is not reached;
- the *Recommendation* is not intended to be a judgment but an opinion as to how the matter should be settled in the best interests of the parties.

The Conciliation Procedure can be used in two situations. First, the Conciliation Procedure obviously applies where particular conditions of contract expressly state it to apply. Second, the parties may choose, although not an original contractual obligation, to adopt the Conciliation Procedure later. The spirit of the Procedure is expressed in rule 2 as follows:

> "This Procedure shall be interpreted and applied in the manner most conducive to the efficient conduct of the proceedings with the primary objective of achieving a settlement of the dispute by agreement between the Parties as quickly as possible."

The object of the Procedure is an expedited result. Rule 4 states the parties will either agree the appointment of a conciliator within 14 days or, in the event of a Presidential appointment, *i.e.* one made by the President of the Institution of Civil Engineers, the appointment should occur within 14 days of a request first being made. Under rule 6, the party requesting the conciliation undertakes to provide the conciliator, immediately following his appointment, and simultaneously to the other party, with any copy Notice of Conciliation together with all relevant copies of Notices of Dispute and other documents which are conditions precedent to conciliation. The instigating party may provide the conciliator (r. 8) with a statement of his views on the dispute and the issues which he wishes to see considered by the conciliator. It is then the conciliator's responsibility to arrange a conciliation meeting with the parties (r. 9). The parties must provide to the conciliator seven days before the conciliation meeting, with copies to the other party, details of the persons who will attend the conciliation meeting together with an indication that those persons have authority to act on behalf of the party (*i.e.* make binding decisions). Rule 10 aims to achieve maximum flexibility in the conduct of the conciliation by permitting the conciliator to take, with the consent of the parties, legal or technical advice. The rule also permits him to investigate the facts and the circumstances of the dispute. The conciliator is permitted, under rule 11, to have independent discussions with either or both of the parties, although confidential information obtained during the course of such meetings may only be released to the other party with the consent of the party making the disclosure to the conciliator. Rules 14–17 deal with the question of reaching agreement. Under rule 14 the conciliator may assist the parties in the preparation of an agreement setting out the terms of settlement, while rule 15 recognises the possibility that the parties will be so polarised that settlement cannot be achieved. Rule 15 of the Procedure deviates from non-binding forms of ADR. The conciliator is empowered, in the absence of agreement between the parties, to issue a recommendation. The nature of a recommendation is set out in rule 16. This is the conciliator's solution to the dispute, based on the conciliator's opinion as to how the parties can best dispose of the dispute between them. Unlike an arbitrator (except where the parties empower the arbitrator to act as an *amiable compositeur* under section 47(1)(b) Arbitration Act 1996) or a judge, the conciliator can be practical and is not bound to adopt strict principles of law nor give reasons for his recommendation, although the conciliator may within seven days of making his recommendation give reasons for it. Rule 17 deals with the question of the conciliator's fees and disbursements which, unless there has been a separate agreement between the parties, should be a joint and several responsibility of the parties to be paid within seven days of the receipt of the account. Receipt of payment means despatch by the conciliator to the parties of his recommendation. This is broadly similar to the release of an arbitrator's award.

The conciliator may review and revise his recommendation, subject to payment of additional fees by the parties. An important provision is found in rule 19 which permits the conciliator to participate in subsequent arbitration proceedings as arbitrator, provided that the parties agree. This allows the conciliator to become involved in a form of Med-Arb, discussed in Chapter 7. Importantly, and quite properly, the conciliator cannot be a witness for either of the parties in any subsequent litigation or arbitration. The one remaining provision of some note in the Conciliation Procedure is rule 21, which overcomes the question of experts/adjudicators and persons of similar status not enjoying, at least at common law, an equivalent immunity to that of judges and arbitrators. As experts or adjudicators (including conciliators) are, excepting those appointed as construction industry adjudicators in accordance with the Housing Grants Construction and Regeneration Act 1996 (section 108(3)), potentially liable to those who employ them for negligence or breach of contract claims, rule 21 acts as an exclusion of liability.

ICC Conciliation Rules

The spirit of the ICE Conciliation Procedure has much in common with the ICC Rules of Conciliation, which are of significance in the resolution of international disputes. Those Rules are set out in a brisk no nonsense manner. According to the Preamble:

> "Settlement is a desirable solution for business disputes of an international character."

The resolution of disputes is by a single conciliator appointed by the International Chamber of Commerce (Art. 1) with any conciliation commenced by the party requesting conciliation applying to the Secretariat at the International Court of Arbitration "setting out succinctly the purpose of the request and accompanying it with the fee required to open the file". Once more, as under the ICE Conciliation Procedure, the aim is to offer expedited resolution, although under Article 3 the party being requested to agree to conciliate the dispute is given a period of 15 days to inform the Secretariat whether or not he agrees to the conciliation option. Once it is settled the parties will attempt to achieve a resolution of their dispute by conciliation, the Secretary General of the International Court of Arbitration appoints a conciliator who informs the parties of his appointment and sets time limits for the presentation by each of the parties of their respective cases. The process is extra-judicial, although Article 5 allows each of the parties to be assisted, if they so wish, by their lawyer. However, the guiding principle behind the conciliation process is that the conciliator is master of his own procedures provided that he operates within the principles of impartiality, equity and justice.

There are three methods by which conciliation will come to an end:

- If the parties sign a settlement agreement which will be final and binding upon them and will remain confidential unless its execution or application require it to be disclosed.
- Upon the production by the conciliator of a report noting that the conciliation has failed.
- If one or other of the parties notifies the conciliator at some stage during the conciliation procedure that he no longer has any desire or wish to participate.

Under Article 9 the parties are responsible in equal shares for the conciliation fees which will be fixed by the Secretariat of the International Court of Arbitration. On it becoming reasonably apparent that the sum lodged with the Secretariat is no longer adequate, this will be revised by the Secretariat. The parties will be notified accordingly and required to pay additional amounts in equal shares. The parties remain equally responsible for the costs of the conciliation unless, if there is agreement, the parties decide on some other apportionment of the costs. Article 10 deals with the potential problem of Med-Arb. Unless the parties agree, a former conciliator cannot act in any subsequent arbitration or litigation which involves the parties. In addition, as under the ICE Conciliation Procedure, the parties agree not to call the conciliator as a witness in any subsequent litigation or proceedings. Article 11 provides some safeguards so that a judge or arbitrator is not prejudiced in any subsequent proceedings by what has happened during a failed attempt at conciliation. These protections are:

- Any views previously expressed or suggestions made by any party to settle the dispute shall be treated as having been *without prejudice*.
- Proposals made to the conciliator shall not be referred to in the subsequent litigation or arbitration.
- No reference can be made in subsequent litigation or arbitration to the fact that one of the parties indicated that it was ready to accept a proposal for settlement put forward by the conciliator.

UNCITRAL Conciliation Rules

A further well used system of conciliation is provided by the UNCITRAL Conciliation Rules. These consist of 20 Articles. The Rules apply (Art. 1) to any dispute which the parties have agreed shall be resolved in accordance with the UNCITRAL Conciliation Rules provided, of course, that the Rules do not contradict the applicable law in a particular jurisdiction. The process of conciliation is commenced in accordance with the procedures in Article 2. The party requiring conciliation sends a written invitation to the other to conciliate, briefly identifying the matters in dispute. For there to be a conciliation the offer to conciliate must be accepted by the other party and if no reply is received within a period of 30 days (Art. 2.4) this may be treated as a rejection of the invitation to conciliate. The party which originally proposed the conciliation may then elect to inform the other party that the request to conciliate has been withdrawn.

Article 3 states that there will be a single conciliator, although a maximum of three is permitted if the parties so agree. Appointment of a conciliator or conciliators is dealt with in Article 4. If there is a single conciliator, the parties attempt to agree his appointment; if there are two conciliators each party will appoint his own conciliator and in the event that there are three conciliators one conciliator will be appointed by each of the parties and they will endeavour to agree the appointment of the third. Article 4.2 provides for the possible appointment of the conciliator or conciliators by an appointing organisation. Article 5 anticipates that written statements will be submitted to the conciliator with copies of the statements made available to the other party. Under Article 5.2 the conciliator may request further written statements to clarify particular issues together with limited disclosure of relevant documents upon which the parties rely to support their case.

The role of the conciliator is defined in Article 7: the status of the conciliator as an independent neutral who is there to facilitate agreement between the parties is emphasised. He can be flexible in the way he approaches matters (Art. 7.3), while Article 7.4 permits him to be interventionist, making proposals for a settlement of the dispute at any stage during the proceedings. Article 9 again emphasises the flexibility of the Conciliation Rules and allows the conciliator to progress by means of meetings and correspondence or, indeed, telephone attendances on the parties. Information provided to the conciliator during the course of a conciliation remains confidential unless the party imparting the information to the conciliator waives the confidentiality (Art. 12). If the parties are successful in agreeing terms of settlement, Article 13 contains a procedure for reducing those terms to a written form. In this, the conciliator takes the initiative. Whenever he believes that there are terms for a possible settlement he submits them to the parties for their observations and, on receipt of their observations, may revise the terms of possible settlement. Article 13.2 anticipates that any settlement will be reduced to written form, either with or without the assistance of the conciliator. The finalisation of the settlement agreement brings an end to the dispute (Art. 13.3). The settlement agreement is binding as between the parties, provided it is a legal document properly drawn up. Subject to the jurisdiction of a particular country, it may be enforced in the courts of that jurisdiction. Article 15 allows for the termination of conciliation proceedings. These may terminate in four situations:

- By the signing of a settlement agreement.
- When it becomes clear that the conciliation process has failed and it cannot be revived.
- By a written declaration from the parties to the conciliator to the effect that the conciliation proceedings have been terminated.
- If one or other of the parties confirms to the conciliator that the conciliation has been terminated.

The use of the Conciliation Rules acts as a suspension of the right to bring arbitration or litigation proceedings during the period of the conciliation (Art. 16).

The question of costs is considered in Article 17 and, as other conciliation schemes do, the Conciliation Rules allow for the costs, as defined in Article 17.1, to be a joint and several responsibility of the parties (Art. 17.2), unless the liability to meet the conciliator's costs is modified by reason of the settlement agreement. Article 18 makes provision for deposits to be taken by the conciliator as security against his own future costs. Rather than as under other conciliation schemes, which allow for the conciliator, by agreement, to be used as an arbitrator in subsequent proceedings, Article 19 of the Conciliation Rules positively states that the conciliator will have no role in any subsequent proceedings, either as arbitrator, legal representative or witness. Further, in very similar terms to those found in the ICC Rules of Conciliation, Article 20 makes it clear that any proposals, information, etc. which come to light during the course of a conciliation are inadmissible in any subsequent litigation or arbitration.

Disputes review boards

A technique analogous to mediation which has developed on major construction projects is the use of a disputes review board or disputes advisor. On large international construction projects, the use of either a disputes review advisor and/or, more particularly, a disputes review board has become increasingly popular. An advisor, or a board, may be invaluable on major international projects (such as World Bank ones) where there is often a requirement for swift, efficient, binding dispute resolution which is seen by a construction team, possibly drawn from different nationalities, to be impartial.

A disputes review board ordinarily consists of three experts who are appointed when a contract is awarded but before disputes arise. The members are chosen for their knowledge and technical expertise and their suitability for the range of issues likely to be thrown up by the project in question. The experts become involved in the project from the outset and make regular site visits/inspections and have access to project documentation. Both employer and contractor nominate one member of the disputes review board with the third member either agreed by both parties or, in the absence of agreement, nominated by an appointing body. Ordinarily the members of the disputes review board will be copied in on all the contract documents, progress reports and other documents which are relevant to the progress of the works. Once a dispute arises during the construction of the works, which cannot be resolved at site level or by the conventional mechanisms in the contract (e.g. an engineer's decision), the dispute will be referred to the disputes review board. The board will consider the issues raised and, following procedures which can be extremely flexible and tailored to serve the interests of the parties, provide recommendations to employer and contractor. These recommendations can be open to acceptance or rejection by the parties and have binding effect at the expiration of a prescribed number of days. Alternatively, the parties can agree that the recommendations of the disputes review board remain binding, after an initial opportunity to reject them, until substantial or practical completion of the project has been achieved – at which stage they can be opened up through the medium of arbitration.

The use of disputes review boards is relatively new with the first such board apparently used on the Eisenhower Tunnel, Second Bore in Colorado, from 1975–1979. Since that date boards have been employed on more than $3 billion worth of construction in the United States by a wide range of employers. These include the Alaska Power Authority, California Department of Transportation, Massachusetts Water Resources Authority, US Army Corp of Engineers and Washington State Department of Transportation. There is obviously a cost associated with the maintenance and running of a disputes review board and it would appear from US data that a board can cost from $1,000–$2,000 per member, per one day meeting. This depends on the location of the board members to the project, the level of their involvement and their charge-out costs. The total cost of a disputes review board over the life of a contract ranges from 0.04–0.51% of the total contract cost. Based on ten early contracts of which the highest percentage, predictably, related to the least costly contract, the statistic is somewhat unsatisfactory. The average per project has been calculated at 0.17%. It may well be that as contractors become more confident in the capacity of a disputes review board to contain, diffuse and resolve on-site conflict, the costs of maintaining a board are compensated for, at least in part, by contractors eventually submitting lower tender prices which do not need to build in costings for future expensive litigation or arbitration. In the United States, there have been two further developments alongside the growth of disputes review boards. The Technical Committee on Contracting Practices of the Underground Technology Council adopted a contract provision in three parts:

- escrow documents to be used for facilitating financial negotiations;
- a Geotechnical Design Summary Report (GDSR) to establish a base line for differing site conditions; and
- the Disputes Review Board.

The placing of bid documents in escrow includes all the documentation shown in the costs' build-up to the successful tenderer's bid. The documents remain the property of the contractor but they are placed in escrow for the duration of the project and can be consulted by employer and contractor, at the request of either, to assist in negotiating price adjustments for variations, unforeseen ground conditions, etc. Ordinarily the documents will also be available to the members of the disputes review board. The second document, the Geotechnical Design Summary Report, is a statement of the anticipated site conditions which provides a clear bench mark for the identification of different site conditions and changed geotechnical requirements. Usually the Geotechnical Design Summary Report is a contract document containing no terms disclaiming responsibility for any inaccuracy or lack of completeness in it. The Geotechnical Design Summary Report is readily available to the members of the disputes review board for their general assistance.

In the United Kingdom the use of disputes review boards remains relatively uncommon. They have been, and are being used, on highways schemes. However, according to one leading arbitrator/conciliator, with experience of serving on two disputes review boards, he has some reservations about the usefulness of the procedure. On one scheme, the board met on one occasion but without any real comprehension of the nature of the dispute against the backdrop of the project as a whole. For English professionals the most well-known example of a panel to resolve disputes related to disputes arising out of the construction of the Channel Tunnel. There was also a disputes review board in place for the Second Severn Crossing, comprising five people. If they produced a unanimous decision on any dispute, that decision was final and there was no right to go to arbitration in regard to the particular dispute. If the decision was not unanimous, either party could go to arbitration. There was a 28-day time limit for decisions but, in practice, the volume of paperwork submitted with claims by one party resulted in an immediate application by the other party for more time to deal with the claim and thereby extended the period for a decision. The board had no valuation obligations and, if one were required, would need outside assistance.

In the United Kingdom the *Construction Disputes Resolution Group* (CDRG) proposed a clause for the formation of a disputes review board in the following terms:

"• Within 30 days of reaching agreement to enter into this contract the parties shall appoint a Disputes Review Board for the purpose of minimising the time and effort necessary to resolve potential claims and disputes which may arise during the progress of the works.
• The Board shall consist of one member selected by the Employer, one by the Contractor and a third selected by the first two. No member shall be selected who is not acceptable to both parties. If there is

disagreement as to the selection of any member, then after a further 30 days, the selection shall, on the application by either party, be made from persons nominated by the Construction Disputes Resolution Group.

- The Board shall have discretion as to the conduct of its enquiries. The Board shall visit the site of the works at regular intervals, determined in consultation with the parties but will respond to any urgent request to intervene.
- A Board member may resign from the Board. A replacement member shall be appointed in the same manner as provided for in Clause D.2 [not reproduced]
- The fees and expenses of all three members of the Board shall be shared equally by the Employer and the Contractor. The Contractor shall make all payments to Board members within 30 days of the presentation of invoices and shall be reimbursed by the Employer.
- The Employer will provide for each Board member one copy of all contract documents, progress reports and other documents pertinent to the activities of the Board. The Contractor shall provide any further documents in its possession which are equally pertinent.
- The Employer will provide all the needs of the Board to enable it to carry out its site meetings function including local travel arrangements, accommodation, conference facilities, secretarial and copying services.
- If the Contractor objects to any act, decision or directive of the Employer, he shall state in writing to the Employer, clearly and in detail, the basis of the objection. The Employer shall respond in writing within 30 days of its receipt.
- Whilst waiting for the Employer's response and throughout the disputes resolution process, the Contractor shall continue to perform the work and conform to the decision or directive.
- If the Contractor is dissatisfied with the Employer's response and the parties cannot amicably settle their difference, either party may appeal to the Board.
- Each party shall supply to the Board complete documentation of its position in relation to the dispute.
- After the Board has considered the matter before it and has given to each party, in writing, its recommendations, each party shall either accept or reject the recommendations by notifying the other party and the Board within 70 days of their receipt. Failure to submit such notification shall be construed as an acceptance of the recommendations.
- Any dispute between the parties which cannot be resolved by negotiation and the assistance of the Board may be settled by arbitration in accordance with the provisions of this contract. All records of the Board shall be admissible as evidence in the arbitration.
- The duties of the Board may be terminated at any time only by the joint decision of the Employer and the Contactor and upon 30 days' written notice to all Board members."

The procedures to be adopted by any disputes review board are questions to be decided by the parties in conjunction with the potential appointees. However, once a dispute has arisen during on-site construction work, which cannot be otherwise resolved, one possible format for the dispute hearing would be as follows:

- The aggrieved party sets out his position to the board, either by way of an oral statement, or an oral statement based on a previously submitted written document.
- The other party then sets out his opening position.
- The parties then provide more detailed presentations, referring to particular items of evidence that they consider crucial. There is limited scope for cross-examination by the opposing party and by the members of the board to clarify issues and achieve a prompt understanding of the problem.
- Both parties make their concluding remarks.
- The board retires to consider their views and to make recommendations and will comply with a prescribed timetable. The period may be "from four days to a week" depending on the need to hold a hearing. Ordinarily once the board's recommendations have been made known they will be open to instant rejection or acceptance by one or other of the parties, but in the absence of a formal objection being made during a prescribed period, the recommendation will become final and binding upon the parties. On most occasions, the board will strive for unanimity in their decision, but with a three-man board, there is capacity for progressing via a majority finding.

On many schemes, given the relatively high costs of a disputes review board, the use of a single disputes advisor or adjudicator may be preferable. The construction industry is perceived as a prime creator of disputes and a hotbed of litigation and arbitration. Although ADR might appear an attractive response to its ills, legislation in the form of the Housing Grants Construction and Regeneration Act 1996 has given a fillip to adjudication as the 'officially' endorsed alternative to litigation/arbitration. Under section 108(1) of the Act a party to a construction contract (being one for construction work in England, Wales or Northern Ireland, and as defined by sections 104-106 inclusive) has the right to refer disputes under the contract for resolution by adjudication under a procedure complying with the Act. The aim is a rapid decision within a timetable of ideally not more than 42 days from the date of referral. Although bound by the law, the adjudicator is investigative and inquisitorial and probably outside the strict rules of natural justice. The adjudicator's decision remains valid until the dispute is finally resolved by litigation, arbitration or agreement. The legislation came into force on 1st May 1998, supported by a Statutory Instrument, the Scheme for Construction Contracts (England and Wales) Regulations 1998.

Chapter 3

Other Forms of Alternative Dispute Resolution

The Mini-Trial - Executive Tribunal

Each party presents the issues to senior executives of both parties who are often assisted by a *neutral* chairman; sometimes a lawyer but frequently from another discipline. The parties may be, but are not necessarily, represented by lawyers. The chairman, if a lawyer, may advise on the likely outcome of litigation but without any binding authority on the parties. After presentation of the issues, the executives try to negotiate a settlement. If successful, the settlement is often set out in a legally enforceable written document. The mini-trial is not really a trial at all (*e.g.* the legal rules of evidence are usually dispensed with), but a settlement procedure designed to convert a legal dispute back into a business problem. It aims to bring the businessmen on each side of the fence directly into the resolution process in the hope that compromises can be reached. The mini-trial flushes out and clarifies disputes, removing from junior and middle management the opportunity to hoodwink senior management by concealing or distorting the truth by wildly optimistic analyses of the party's position, often exaggerating strengths and playing down weaknesses. To date the technique has been little used in the United Kingdom.

The advantages of a mini-trial are:

- A lengthy hearing is eliminated by its summary conduct.
- Each party's case is professionally presented but without any formal rules of procedure or evidence.
- Those who ultimately decide on whether the dispute should be settled (and, if so, on what terms) have the opportunity to be guided by a person with some degree of prestige and outside objectivity.
- The presentations are made to, and the ultimate decision made by, persons with the requisite authority to commit to settlement the bodies which they represent.

- The use of senior executives from the organisations in dispute who can then act subsequently as negotiators, if necessary. It brings to the process of dispute resolution people who can provide a *fresh* mind. Their lack of previous involvement in the project or transaction giving rise to the dispute is a positive feature in that they have none of the prejudices and the false adoption of positions of those whose performance during the course of the actual contract may have been at fault and who may now wish to conceal previous ineptitude.
- Organisations which may have made a long-term investment in co-operation and which have a number of complex interlinking business transactions can identify common interests which need to be preserved.
- The use of senior company personnel on the mini-trial panel means that dispute resolution is managed by those who are usually well acquainted with trade customs and practice and technical matters arising both from the questions in dispute and the general organisation of the particular industry.

The disadvantages include:

- Possible over-simplification of complicated technical and legal issues.
- One party may have no real interest in settling and will simply use the process to string the other along.
- Mini-trials are not appropriate for disputes which turn on the credibility of personnel. The mini-trial, with minimal recourse to the assessment and testing of evidence by cross-examination and the substantial use of written statements to provide direct testimony, is ill-suited for the verification of the accuracy of what is stated or to assess the veracity of particular individuals.
- As with other forms of non-binding ADR, the process is likely to fail whenever a particular party has no real desire to settle, procedural advantages of the *White Book* or the *Green Book* favour one of the parties, or the law is decidedly weighted in favour of one of the parties.
- The level of senior management time which needs to be invested in the mini-trial may not render the process cost-effective for the smaller dispute.

The first recognised mini-trial is said to have been between TRW and Telecredit Inc[1] to resolve a dispute concerning infringement of a computer terminal patent in 1977. In the particular case, the mini-trial was not used early in the dispute-resolution process. The parties had already reached the stage of discovery and major negotiations had occurred. Apparently each of the parties had spent in excess of $500,000. Faced with the enormous costs of continued litigation and the potential futility of such a process to the loser, the parties' representatives decided the following:

- No further discovery would occur except that which was necessary for the mini-trial. They agreed to take summary witness statements which could be amplified, if necessary, at a later date.
- The period for discovery and preparation for the mini-trial would be no longer than six weeks, with any dispute about discovery which occurred during that period submitted to the neutral adviser for his non-binding advice.
- To make the appointment of their mini-trial chairman from a range of possible candidates which included a former Supreme Court Justice and a former Deputy Attorney General of the United States. In the end the appointee was known for his expertise in patent law.
- To share the fees and expenses of the neutral chairman with the fees to be assessed against the eventual losing party if settlement was not reached and a trial resulted.
- The nature of the material to be submitted to the neutral chairman before the mini-trial.
- All exhibits relied upon by the parties were to be submitted in advance to the other party and also to the neutral chairman.
- The parties were to present written opening statements in advance.
- The chairman could submit written questions to the parties' technical experts in advance of the mini-trial.
- Rules of evidence were to be discarded, although each party was expected to act in good faith.

---

1 *The Manager's Guide to Resolving Legal Disputes - Better Results Without Litigation,* James F. Henry and Jethro K. Lieberman, Harper & Row, New York, 1985, Chap. 3, pp. 19-25

- There was to be unlimited scope to decide the material to be placed before the mini-trial panel. The chairman could ask clarifying questions but was not permitted to curtail particular lines of presentation.
- The mini-trial procedure was to be outside the litigation system and no applications to the courts were possible. What was prepared for the mini-trial in written format was not to be admissible at any subsequent trial.
- The chairman could not participate in any subsequent proceedings.
- If either party attempted to make applications to the courts or to call the neutral chairman as a witness, that party would be required to pay the entire costs of the neutral's fees and expenses for the mini-trial irrespective of the outcome of the trial.
- Each side was granted equal time to put its argument and to make a speech in rebuttal of what was submitted by the opposing party. Time was apportioned as follows:

  – opening presentation by Telecredit – 4 hours
  – rebuttal statement by TRW – 1 1/2 hours
  – further rebuttal statement by Telecredit – 1/2 hour
  – question and answer session – 1 hour
  – TRW – 4 hours to present its case
  – Telecredit rebuttal statement – 1 1/2 hours
  – further rebuttal statement by TRW – 1/2 hour
  – question and answer session - 1 hour

- The presentations were mostly made by lawyers but once the mini-trial was at an end the lawyers played no part in the settlement talks between senior management.
- If senior management were unable to negotiate a suitable settlement, the chairman was empowered to provide an advisory opinion on the possible outcome of litigation.
- The chairman's views were non-binding.
- The mini-trial agreement contained a confidentiality clause:

  "Any violation of these rules by either party will seriously prejudice the opposing party and will be *prima facie* grounds for a mistrial or disqualification motion."

Apparently, senior management only took 30 minutes to reach a settlement following the mini-trial procedure.

Another application of the mini-trial procedure was in a product liability dispute between TRW and Automatic Radio. Automatic Radio brought proceedings against TRW alleging that a circuit board assembly purchased from TRW malfunctioned thereby causing radios to fail within a few months of purchase. Automatic Radio had sales of $15,000,000–$18,000,000 in the car radio market. It alleged that it was being squeezed out of the market as a result of the errors. The proposed litigation would have turned on complicated technical issues in relation to the design of circuit boards and workmanship. Also, if successful, Automatic Radio would have needed to have damages assessed. One major concern of the parties was to ensure the confidentiality of the process and to avoid the automatic disclosure of information imparted to the mini-trial panel in subsequent litigation. Since the mini-trial is simply one form of settlement negotiation, there should not be any major legal problems provided both parties act in good faith. TRW and Automatic Radio sensibly addressed the question of confidentiality in the document setting up the mini-trial and included the following clause:

> "1. No transcript or recording shall be made of this proceeding. All aspects of this advisory proceeding, including without limitation, any written material prepared or oral presentations made between or among the parties and/or the advisor for the purposes of this proceeding are confidential to all persons, including the court, as inadmissible in evidence, whether or not for purposes of impeachment, in the pending civil action or in any litigation which directly or indirectly involves the parties. However, evidence which would be otherwise admissible if this advisory proceeding did not take place shall not be rendered inadmissible by its presentation at the advisory proceeding. The advisor will be instructed to treat the subject matter of this proceeding as confidential and refrain from disclosing any of the information exchanged to third parties. The advisor is disqualified as a witness, consultant or expert for either party in this and in any other dispute between the parties. His advisory response, if any, is inadmissible for all purposes in this or in any other dispute involving the parties."

A further leading example in the United States of the use of the mini-trial was the multi-million dollar NASA dispute in 1982, again involving TRW, as well as Space Communications Co. (Spacecom). Pre-trial proceedings had taken place over two years. There was concern that a special tracking and data relay satellite system would not be able to be launched on time. The parties agreed to a mini-trial, met and successfully resolved that dispute and other disputes between them in the space of one week. The mini-trial occupied just one day. One significant feature of the NASA mini-trial was that it involved a government agency which might or might not have had money to pay the costs of the neutral adviser and which was also subject to public auditing considerations. Those problems were overcome and the parties proceeded on the basis of written statements which were exchanged. The mini-trial was held before senior executives. These were the directors of the Goddard Space Flight Center, NASA's associate administrator for tracking data systems; the president of Spacecom and a divisional vice-president of TRW. No witnesses were called and only the four senior executives asked questions.

The mini-trial technique was used in a dispute between Texaco and Borden. In May 1980 Borden Inc. filed a $200 million anti- trust suit against Texaco Inc. over a natural gas contract in Louisiana. The Texaco lawyers produced over 300,000 documents in the course of discovery. A preliminary trial was set simply to interpret the contract. A few weeks before the preliminary trial date, counsel for Borden suggested to Texaco's in-house counsel the use of the mini-trial procedure. The proposal was that each lawyer be allowed one hour to present his case in front of the executive vice-presidents of each company. Each party was represented by technical advisers assisted by a third-party neutral. The issues were resolved over a two-week period following the information exchange. The parties negotiated a new gas supply contract that had not been in issue in the original case.

Similar techniques were used in a dispute between Wisconsin Electric Power Company and American Can. American Can sued for $41 million for breach of contract relating to industrial waste sold to Wisconsin Electric as boiler fuel. Wisconsin Electric counterclaimed for $20 million for the excess cost of burning the waste. The technical issues were obviously complex. A judge was selected as a third-party neutral and there were three days for case submissions. The judge gave his views on the likely outcome of the dispute. Settlement was achieved after a three-month period. It has been estimated that the parties saved at least 75 days of trial, many months of protracted discovery and inspection of documents and even more substantial advisers' fees.

Other notable uses of the mini-trial[2] have been in disputes involving US federal contracts. Yarn quotes the example of the US

---

2 "Mini-Trial", Douglas H. Yarn, ADR *A Practical Guide to Resolve Construction Disputes,* American Arbitration Association, 1994, p. 233-245 at p. 234

Army Corps of Engineers' first mini-trial which concerned an acceleration claim pending before the Armed Services Board of Contract Appeals (ASBCA). The $630,000 claim was apparently settled in three days for $380,000. The Corps' second mini-trial dealt with a $55.6 million claim involving changed site conditions in the construction of the Tennesee Tombigee Waterway. This mini-trial lasted three days, was followed by another one-day mini-trial and produced a settlement of $17.2 million. A further example, cited by Yarn, is that of a mini-trial at the Atlanta office of the American Arbitration Association. This involved a $6 million claim and counter-claim arising out of the construction of a paper manufacturing plant. The mini-trial panel, composed of a retired federal judge and two senior executives, combined a two-day proceeding with subsequent negotiations over several months. This led to ultimate settlement.

One of the great problems with all forms of ADR, including the mini-trial, is to decide when the process should be initiated. As the mini-trial is a non-binding form of dispute resolution its value will ordinarily be assessed by the parties and their lawyers at some stage prior to formal litigation or arbitration. However, the true value of the mini-trial may not be apparent until the precise nature of the dispute is known and it is therefore possible that the mini-trial will be most effective once the dispute has arisen, formal litigation commenced and pleadings exchanged. This creates a problem: once formal litigation or arbitration have been commenced it is difficult to deviate (a process that the lawyers do not assist) towards a process which is non-adversarial and based on the long-term benefits of compromise. It may well be impossible for the parties themselves to take the giant step necessary to initiate the mini-trial procedure, in which event it may be more appropriate for the party supportive of ADR to use the services of one of the ADR organisations, such as CEDR or the Chartered Institute of Arbitrators, to moot the possibilities offered by the mini-trial in the mind of the opposing party.

As there is little experience in the United Kingdom of the use of the mini-trial, it is difficult to have any hard and fast ideas about the composition of the panel drawn from domestic data. It is therefore attractive to look to the United States which does have experience of the use of the mini-trial procedure. It is no good choosing the executives simply on the basis of experience. They need to be good listeners, quick witted, prepared to make concessions when they see their own side's case exposed warts and all, accomplished in putting fact finding questions, as opposed to making speeches. They must also have sufficient authority within their organisation to make binding decisions and other necessary compromises. The choice of the neutral chairman poses different questions. The tendency may be to appoint a legal personality, who will have organisational skills, keep the process moving efficiently and have experience of the area of law in question. This is particularly important if the third-party neutral is to advise the parties on the potential outcome of litigation. The legal chairman may be disadvantaged if the parties wish to discuss what the best settlement option would be and discussions get bogged down in technical details. The American experience is that parties have shown a preference for retired judges as the third-party chairman in mini-trials.

Although it is on occasions better for the parties to devise their own mini-trial procedure, in the United States both the CPR Institute for Dispute Resolution, formerly The Center for Public Resources, and the American Arbitration Association have published their own mini-trial procedures. Similarly, in the United Kingdom, the Chartered Institute of Arbitrators has had a mini-trial procedure since 1990. *The Chartered Institute of Arbitrators Guidelines for Supervised Settlement Procedure* (reproduced at Appendix 11) indicate:

> "Most *bona fide* disputes between reputable parties are capable of settlement in a manner that is business orientated, thus avoiding or at least curtailing legal expenditure, loss of executive time and the deterioration of valuable business relationships.
> Such a settlement can be facilitated by the use of a structured procedure which ensures that authorised management representatives are presented with the facts, viewed from both sides, and can then enter into negotiations under the guidance of a neutral adviser experienced in conciliation, mediation and arbitration techniques."

Following what are described as the *Explanatory Notes*, there are five rules. These are: rule 1, the procedure; rule 2, exchange of information; rule 3, the formal meeting; rule 4, negotiations; rule 5, costs. Helpfully the pamphlet concludes with a draft Agreement for parties embarking upon a mini-trial. In the United States, the CPR Institute for Dispute Resolution has devised[3] a mediation procedure and a mini-trial programme building on the experience of earlier

---

3 CPR Model Mediation Procedure for Business Disputes in Europe and CPR Model Mini-Trial Procedure for Business Disputes in Europe 1996

versions. The latter is somewhat more sophisticated than that produced by the Chartered Institute of Arbitrators. The model mini-trial procedure comprises both the rules and a written agreement for the commencement of a mini-trial proceeding. The rules cover the appointment of the neutral adviser (r.2); the exchange of information between the parties and to the neutral third party (r.3) (ordinarily not more than 25 pages double-spaced A4 sized paper); negotiations between the management representatives (r.5); confidentiality (r.6); and court proceedings (r.7). Some of the rules merit more detailed consideration. For instance, rule 3.2.1 emphasises that there must be an element of cards on the table from the parties. However, excessive discovery, as found in litigation, is to be avoided. It is therefore the parties' responsibility to endeavour in good faith to agree on appropriate and necessary discovery. Rule 4.3 emphasises that each party has the opportunity to present his best case with the other side being entitled to make a rebuttal. The order and length of presentations and rebuttals is a matter for agreement as stated in the Initiating Agreement. Flexibility is permitted in the format that presentations and rebuttals should take. The procedure allows for the use of witnesses of fact and expert witnesses (r.4.4). The mini-trial panel is permitted to put questions to those appearing before them to clarify issues, although the strict rules of evidence do not apply. Apart from informal notes, the procedure has no record taken of it (r.4.5). The subsequent negotiations are covered in Rule 5 which indicates (r.5.3) that an appropriate written agreement is signed as soon as agreement has been reached. Rule 6.1 guarantees the confidentiality of the process.

In line with other dispute-resolution schemes, rule 6.2 makes it clear that the neutral adviser cannot play any role in subsequent litigation or arbitration. The use of the mini-trial procedure also acts as a block on the commencement of litigation until the process has been exhausted and, questionable in the United Kingdom, suspends operation of the limitation periods. The procedure comes to an end under rule 9 if the parties fail to execute a written settlement agreement on or before the 30th day following conclusion of the Formal Meeting held under Rule 4, subject to agreed extensions, or if either party serves on the other and on the neutral adviser a written notice withdrawing from the proceedings. As with most other dispute-resolution schemes, the neutral adviser cannot be sued: he is protected by rule 11.

Rent-a -Judge

This system has been popular in California for some time, particularly in Los Angeles. It was a reaction to the long periods required to bring actions to trial and was a development of the litigation system rather than a truly ADR technique. It also relies upon two particular features of Californian law. Section 638 of the Code of Civil Procedure states that upon agreement of the parties the court can "appoint a referee to try any or all of the issues in an action or proceedings whether of fact or of law". Once the judge has designated a particular person to hear the case as referee, that person decides the date and place of a hearing and exercises all the usual powers of a trial judge. The procedure then adopted is exactly the same as that used in Californian trial courts. The court reporter is present and a record made. The referee must make his findings in writing to the court within 20 days of the hearing, stating his findings of fact and conclusions on the interpretation of the law. These findings then become findings of the court and judgment is entered as if the action had been tried in the conventional way. The parties have the right to appeal the referee's decision. The appeal may be either by motion to set aside the referee's report and to ask for a new trial in the lower court or an appeal to the appellate courts upon matters of law.

Another feature of Californian law is Article 6, section 21 of the Constitution. Under this provision the court may order the case to be tried by a temporary judge who is a member of the state Bar, "sworn in and empowered to act until the final determination of the case". A temporary judge has all the powers of an ordinary judge, including the power to commit someone for contempt. The advantage of the constitutional procedure over the statutory one is privacy. The court record will only contain a reference to the appointment of the temporary judge to try the issue in a statement of his decision. There is no requirement for a detailed report which will be made to the court, and thereby, become part of the record.

CEDR has launched its own *Judicial Appraisal Scheme*[4] as a form of rent-a-judge which is distinct from the Californian model and does not use judges in a litigation role. It draws upon the expertise of senior counsel and former judges in developing the role of ADR in

---

4 15th July 1993

the United Kingdom. Members of the Scheme include former High Court judges who offer a fast-track approach by which actual or potential litigants can seek an independent assessment of their case by a joint presentation to the senior lawyers on the CEDR Panel. Parties can then choose to go on to better informed negotiations or to mediate a settlement. Users of the Scheme can agree to treat the assessment as binding. Alternatively, users can use the assessment as a means to assist in the management of cases through the streamlining of issues for future trial or to influence the question of legal costs awards. The English scheme has grown out of models first adopted by the American Judicial and Arbitration and Mediation Services, Inc. (JAMS) which was founded in 1979 and developed a panel of approximately 200 former American judges. JAMS came to preside over approximately 10,000 cases annually in 20 or so offices in the United States, becoming big business with a revenue of over $20,000,000 in 1992. Its Marketing Director attributed its 90% success rate to the former judges' credibility and experience of evaluating facts and legal principles without losing their neutrality. Other major US players include ENDISPUTE.

Other ADR Techniques

There are a number of other ADR techniques or refinements of techniques already discussed which are more developed in the United States than in the United Kingdom or which are yet to produce a distinctive English version.[5] These include:

The New Jersey Medical Practice Mini-Trial
This has been used for medical malpractice cases in New Jersey where liability is admitted. The insurance company and the claimant select a retired judge to listen to a short presentation of the case with witnesses being heard if necessary. At the end of the presentation, the judge provides the parties with his assessment of quantum. Apparently his advice nearly always results in a settlement given that under New Jersey procedures the retired judge's decision is admissible in court.

---

5 These are usefully summarised in *Corporate Counsel's Primer on Alternative Dispute Resolution Techniques*, William A. Hancock, Business Laws Inc, 1990, para.401

The Confidential Listener Mediation

The parties designate a confidential listener and tell him their maximum and minimum settlement figures. There is agreement that if these numbers overlap, they simply settle the case by splitting the difference. If the numbers do not overlap the listener reports this to the parties, and they can try the process again.

The Century City Mini-Trial

This developed in west Los Angeles and is a modification of the simple mini-trial. It relies on summary arguments by both parties to a three-person panel. The panel consists of the highest ranking officers of the two opposing companies with an impartial presiding officer, usually a retired judge. After the arguments are presented, the two company officers try to agree on settlement. If they cannot, the presiding officer renders an oral or written opinion on what he believes the decision would be if he were to settle the matter as a judge. This may serve to focus minds on the desirability or otherwise of any litigation.

Mini-Trial by Contract

Instead of simply agreeing to use the mini-trial procedure after a dispute has arisen, parties may agree, as they would agree an arbitration clause, to make provision for a mini-trial as a condition precedent to any litigation. Hancock refers[6] to advice given by an American law professor in a particular case. Each party to the contract was asked to designate an appropriate company officer at subsidiary vice-president rank to whom any disputes would be referred. If the second-tier corporate executives could not resolve the problem, they would by agreement refer it to their respective chief executive officers for another attempt at amicable resolution. If that failed, the parties could then litigate. The same law professor has also suggested that a provision might be considered which required each party to participate in good faith in a standard mini-trial with some type of monetary penalty against a party which lost a mini-trial, commenced legal proceedings and was still unsuccessful.

MEDALOA™ [7]

This combines mediation with last-offer arbitration. Whenever a dispute involves a question of value or a monetary claim, parties may

---

6 *ibid.* para. 401.019

7 MEDALOA™, Mediation and Last Offer Arbitration, American Arbitration Association

submit their last demand and last offer to a neutral arbitrator who is simply authorised to select one or the other. The American Arbitration Association proposes two possible clauses for use by parties to achieve this:

> "The parties hereby submit the following monetary dispute to mediation administered by the American Arbitration Association under its Commercial Mediation Rules and if unable to agree on a settlement amount, they agree to submit their dispute to a neutral person appointed by the AAA who shall select between their final negotiated positions, that selection being binding upon the parties."

An alternative clause reads:

> "If a monetary dispute arises out of or relating to this contract, the parties agree to first submit it to mediation administered by the American Arbitration Association under its Commercial Mediation Rules and, if unable to agree upon a settlement amount, to submit their dispute to a neutral person appointed by the AAA who shall select between their final negotiated positions, that selection being binding upon the parties."

The American Arbitration Association suggests that MEDALOA may be the answer to the problems of Med-Arb:[8]

> "MEDALOA may be preferable to a similar process called Med-Arb which combines mediation with binding arbitration, because Medaloa limits the arbitrator to selecting between the last offers of the parties. Medaloa encourages parties to continue negotiating."

---

8 *ibid.*, p. 6

Chapter 4

Mediation-Arbitration (Med-Arb)

Some UK lawyers denigrate mediation and other non-binding ADR techniques simply because they are non-binding. They suggest these techniques are a weak response to the need for prompt and efficient dispute resolution and send out the wrong message about how a claimant sees his case. Many American lawyers do not share this view. In one American survey, 85% of those polled did not believe that to propose ADR was a sign of weakness.[1]

One method of addressing concerns about the non-binding nature of mediation is the hybrid technique of med-arb. Its purpose is to commit the parties, usually through a clause in their contract, to continue the ADR processes in a manner which will ensure *resolution of the dispute.* It is a way of having the best of both worlds. Med-arb recognises arbitration still has an important role to play in the resolution of commercial disputes where an imposed decision may be essential.

Med-arb recognises that mediation may not resolve all the issues between the parties but limits the arbitration solely to the intractable disputes, thereby bringing a cost and time saving to the parties. Assume the disputants will first attempt to negotiate a settlement. If that fails they will embark upon mediation and if no agreement (or only partial agreement) is reached the mediator will change roles and become an arbitrator empowered to impose a binding decision on the parties. Many doubts have been expressed, particularly by lawyers. Does med-arb inevitably compromise the neutral's capacity legally to act in an adjudicative capacity while at the same time undermining the efficacy of the initial mediation - where the mediator should seek to create an atmosphere of trust and a willingness to impart confidences to him in the caucus sessions? It has been suggested that, practically speaking, the mediator/arbitrator can fulfil both roles if he provides the parties with a report at the end of the caucus sessions detailing what was said during them. That is

---

1 "Quiet resolution brews for settling disputes", Rob McManamey, ENR, 26th August 1991, pp. 21-23

not entirely convincing. The problem remains that such a cards on the table approach may not encourage parties to be open at the mediation stage, particularly if they are likely to reveal their bottom line positions to the mediator. There are other practical considerations. If the parties agree, during the original contract negotiations, that they will use a form of med-arb for the resolution of any disputes which arise, it may be difficult to assess when the mediation phase should give way to the arbitral one. Simply to place the responsibility on the mediator to advise the parties when mediation should give way to arbitration may be an inadequate response.

The value of med-arb is difficult to assess. The technique has not been greatly used in the United Kingdom and there is an absence of recorded data. Even in the United States, with its far longer track record of ADR generally, information is scant. Douglas H. Yarn concludes[2]:

> "For all practical purposes there have been comparatively few detailed reports of Med/Arb applications in construction disputes. Therefore, most of the available commentary about these hybrid processes is both anecdotal and speculative."

It is reasonably safe to assume a similar picture would emerge in other industries.

In his footnote Yarn states:[3]

> "One proponent estimates '[t]here are probably thousands of cases...' However, his [the proponent's] definition is so broad as to include the informal use of any third party engaged to render an opinion, binding or non-binding, after failing to mediate a resolution. C.J. Gnaedinger *Mediation-Arbitration: Keeping Conflicts Out of Court*, The Construction Specifier, 54 (1985)."

David C. Elliott[4] refers to three successful uses of med-arb in the United States:

- A multi-million dollar dispute between IBM and Fujitsu.
- An environmental clean-up dispute between Conoco Inc. and Browning Ferris Industries over removal of hazardous

---

2 "Med/Arb", *ADR A Practical Guide to Resolving Construction Disputes*, American Arbitration Association, 1994, p. 217
3 *ibid.*, p. 225
4 "Med/arb: Fraught with danger or ripe with opportunity?" (1996) 62, *JCI Arb.*3, 175, p.176

chemicals. Three years of litigation gave way to nine months of mediation. This resolved most of the issues but did not finally settle liability. The mediator then became an arbitrator.

- Federal Deposit Insurance Corporation and Chery, Bekart and Holland was a claim for auditors' negligence concerning a defaulting bank. After $2 million of litigation costs, without getting to trial, the parties successfully used a med-arb technique.

If mediation fails the mediator's subsequent appointment as arbitrator of the same dispute is superficially attractive. When played out like High Court litigation, and subject to any cultural and actual changes the Arbitration Act 1996 may bring, arbitration is expensive and lengthy. Most arbitrators charge an hourly rate, often with substantial cancellation fees if the arbitration settles at any stage before a full hearing. Further, once a dispute blows up into a full arbitration, hordes of lawyers and expert witnesses appear to glide effortlessly onto the stage. Anything that may lessen ultimate costs must seem a good idea to the parties. An arbitrator, already well acquainted with the facts by reason of a recently completed, although unsuccessful, mediation, does not have the same learning curve as an appointee coming fresh to the dispute. Such a neutral will have acquired a greater awareness of the dispute than would a conventional arbitrator and is likely to have revealed some of his own impressions as to the weaknesses and strengths of a party's case during the caucus sessions. This might assist parties more easily to draw conclusions as to how a mediator would make a final award in arbitration and, with the issues more clearly delineated, encourage them to abandon their weaker arguments and deploy simpler arbitration procedures than they would in a conventional arbitration where the arbitrator has to be educated as to the nuances of each party's case, and good and bad points are pursued with equal vigour. Perhaps the parties may already have prepared detailed position papers for the mediation – comprising narrative, supporting documents and expert opinion, and these may adequately stand as Statements of Case for the arbitral stage. When sitting as an arbitrator, the former mediator may simply need to interview the parties, acting inquisitorially, to clarify the outstanding issues in his own mind so as to draft a final award.

The question arises – does the Arbitration Act 1996 with its twin emphases on party autonomy and the tribunal being the master of its own procedures assist med-arb? Obviously the 1996 Act will not affect the mediation phase but, provided there is a written arbitration agreement for the purposes of section 5 of the Act (a looser definition than that under section 32 of the 1950 Act), it will be the regulatory framework for the arbitral stage.

Of the so-called "general principles" stated in section 1 of the 1996 Act, (a) states:

> "the object of arbitration is to obtain the fair resolution of disputes by an impartial tribunal without unnecessary delay or expense;"

The cynical bystander may suggest that med-arb fails at the first hurdle. A former mediator, having heard each side's presentation and perhaps favoured one side over the other for legal reasons or because of the dictates of *fairness* and *justice* (even if no views have been expressed to the parties), might not even pass the first necessary test.

The overriding duty of the arbitral tribunal is found in section 33 of the 1996 Act. This states:

> "(1) The tribunal shall -
>
> (a) act fairly and impartially as between the parties, giving each party a reasonable opportunity of putting his case and dealing with that of his opponent, and
>
> (b) adopt procedures suitable to the circumstances of the particular case, avoiding unnecessary delay or expense, so as to provide a fair means for the resolution of the matters falling to be determined.
>
> (2) The tribunal shall comply with that general duty in conducting the arbitral proceedings, in its decisions on matters of procedure and evidence and in the exercise of all other powers conferred on it."

Arbitrators are to have regard both to the interests of justice and efficiency. They are not duty bound to adopt procedures akin to those set out in the Rules of the Supreme Court and should use the flexibility arbitration provides to tailor the procedures to meet the needs of the parties. The key words in section 33(1)(a) of the 1996 Act are "giving each party a reasonable opportunity of putting his case and dealing with that of his opponent ...". It is arguable that a former mediator, now sitting as an arbitrator, having heard the parties' confidential positions cannot comply with the second limb of section 33(1)(a).

Under the Arbitration Act 1996 the powers to regulate the conduct of specific references are found in section 34. Importantly, the statute does not claim to set out a definitive list, with sub-section (2) of section 34 containing the words "Procedural and evidential matters include ...". Sub-paragraphs (e) and (g) of subsection (2) give arbitrators important powers. They permit the tribunal to take the lead in establishing the facts and essentially provide for an inquisitorial approach which may assist med-arb. The arbitrator might follow up and examine themes first raised in the mediation phase. Continental Europe has used an inquisitorial system for generations. Under such a system the judge or arbitrator is investigative. He is not there merely to assess the evidence having allowed each party to produce its evidence and cross-examine the opponent's witnesses (sometimes extremely crossly).

Again, sub-paragraph (f) will be of interest to supporters of med-arb in that arbitrators are now expressly permitted to dispense with the strict rules of evidence, if appropriate in all the circumstances. Whether it permits an arbitrator to go further than the Civil Evidence Act 1995 or to put himself in breach of the principles of natural justice are moot points.

Again, med-arb is potentially assisted by section 46 (1)(b) of the 1996 Act (closely modelled on Art. 28 of the UNCITRAL Model Law) which permits the arbitrator to act, with the consent of the parties, as an *amiable compositeur* and reach decisions *ex aequo et bono*[5]. The extent to which this allows the parties to contract out of the principles of natural justice is debatable given the tribunal's general duties under section 33 of the Act.

In their commentary on the 1996 Act,[6] Rutherford and Sims refer to Stewart Boyd QC's Bernstein Lecture in 1989 when he said:

> " The fact that arbitration, unlike the courts, depends for its vigour on market forces, and the market in which English arbitration operates is an international market where equity clauses are almost universally recognised, if London will not accommodate equity clauses (and I believe it can), Alsatia undoubtedly will."

In fact, English courts would now, in all likelihood, look sympathetically at equity clauses regardless of earlier contrary references in case law.[7]

It may be that express statutory recognition of equity clauses may assist the mediator/arbitrator. Acting with the parties consent, which

---

5 Such clauses are discussed in Mustill & Boyd, *Commercial Arbitration*, (2nd ed.), Butterworths, 1989, pp. 74-86
6 *The Arbitration Act 1996: A Practical Guide*, FT Law & Tax, 1996, pp. 158-9
7 *Channel Tunnel* v *Balfour Beatty* [1993] AC 334

med-arb would require, under section 46(1)(b), as strict requirements of law have been discarded, there could be no possible grounds to operate the appeals' procedure under the 1996 Act[8]. The status of so-called equity clauses is not free from doubt in case law. In *Home and Overseas Insurance Co* v *Mentor Insurance Co* [9] Parker LJ said:

> " I have no hesitation in accepting the submission of Counsel for Home that a clause which purported to free arbitrators to decide without regard to the law and according, for example, to their own notions of what would be fair would not be a valid arbitration clause."

Finally, there is some debate as to the interpretation to be placed on section 48 of the Act. Sub-section (1) states:

> "The parties are free to agree on the powers exercisable by the arbitral tribunal as regards remedies."

Subject to further definition by the courts, it is arguable that the word, "remedies", as used in sub-section (1) permits the parties to agree that the solution imposed by the arbitrator may extend beyond those available at law and encompass a med-arb approach.

Even if the Arbitration Act 1996 eases the legal difficulties, merely to follow a clarion call that med-arb is attractive is too superficial a response. It may be that the mediation phase has resolved most, but not all, issues and it seems, in the euphoria of partial resolution, appropriate to permit the neutral to reach a binding decision on the outstanding ones. The realisation that the mediator is subsequently authorised to adjudicate, if necessary, may make med-arb more effective at producing a negotiated settlement than mediation alone. But mediation, unlike litigation or arbitration, succeeds above all because it is based on communication and trust. A mediator is not constrained to accept one party's case at the expense of rejecting the other party's. The mediation process is designed to release the parties from positional bargaining, frequently articulated as the law's promotion of the establishment of rights, and to look for solutions by a re-focus on interests. With the respect and confidence of both parties, the mediator can listen to the parties communicating confidentially their real positions in the dispute and what they honestly want to achieve. A good mediator will assist the parties in looking for and achieving solutions by identifying what a party really

---

8 Ss 68-69 Arbitration Act 1996
9 [1989], 13 All ER 74, p. 80

wants. Mediation, founded on a lack of coercion, allows the parties to agree without judicial imposition. The process straddles the law by providing flexible solutions in the form of trade-offs and the recognition of mutual gains which the law, perhaps with the exception of section 46(1)(b) of the Arbitration Act 1996, is unable to provide.

In choosing to ignore that mediation is consensual and extra-judicial, whereas arbitration remains by and large confrontational and part of the legal process, perhaps the hybrid med-arb, although well intentioned, is seriously flawed. Because of pressures on his time a busy arbitrator might coerce the parties during the mediation stage into a settlement which the parties might not desire. Again, knowing that the mediator might subsequently act as their arbitrator, the parties may be encouraged to be less forthcoming. A lazy or inexperienced neutral might cause problems and be inclined to move prematurely to the arbitration phase whenever there was an apparent impasse in the mediation. Influenced by the information released in the mediation, the mediator's subsequent award, when sitting as arbitrator, might owe more to knowledge gained during the mediation (communicated by one party during the caucus sessions and unknown to the other party) than to that admitted in the arbitration phase under the rules of evidence. Regardless of any protestations to the contrary, it is difficult, if not impossible, for any neutral to disregard the parties' confidential compromise positions for settlement expressed during the mediation phase and yet then have to turn round and make a non-compromising award based upon legally assessed rights incorporated in a reasoned award.

Neither practical nor legal difficulties have prevented med-arb clauses being proposed and adopted in the United States construction industry. A simple clause would read:[10]

> "Any and all disputes that arise out of or relate to this agreement, or the performance or breach thereof, shall be subject first to mediation in good faith by the parties administered by the American Arbitration Association under its Construction Industry Mediation Rules, before resorting to arbitration. Thereafter, any remaining unresolved controversy or claim arising out of or relating to this agreement, or the performance or breach thereof, shall be settled by arbitration administered by the American Arbitration Association under its Construction Industry Arbitration Rules, and judgment on the award rendered by the arbitrator may be entered in any court having jurisdiction thereof. The sole arbitrator shall

---

10 *ADR A Practical Guide to Resolving Construction Disputes*, American Arbitration Association, 1994, p. 226

be the same person as the mediator who is selected under the applicable mediation rules."

In the United States a number of modifications have sought to address the difficulties posed by med-arb in its basic form where a single neutral is used who may be accused of lacking impartiality or independence. Under the first, med-then-arb, the mediator and subsequent arbitrator are different individuals. The arbitrator, who is not privy to the mediation phase, will not be influenced by the discussions and materials relating to the previous unsuccessful mediation. Although it solves the problem of having the same individual, it adds time and cost to the dispute-resolution process. The appointee as arbitrator has the same learning curve as any other arbitrator. In an attempt to reduce the additional cost the arbitrator may be pre-selected at the commencement of the mediation and at least sit in during the open session presentations to the mediator. The obvious downside is that the parties will have to pay for the arbitrator's time spent in the mediation phase. Although the technique may have some merit, where the parties are reasonably confident not all the issues will be resolved in the mediation, ultimately it is unattractive because it may cause the mediation joint sessions to be conducted in a more adversarial manner simply to impress the arbitrator.

In the United States the Deep Foundations Construction Industry Roundtable has recommended med-then-arb and adoption of the following clause:[11]

> "Coverage. The parties agree to submit all claims, disputes or controversies arising out of, or in relation to, the interpretation, application or enforcement of this agreement, including dispute resolution procedures, to sequential mandatory discussions, mediation and arbitration for resolution of all disputes before, and as a condition precedent to self-help, arbitration, judicial action or other remedies. This mandatory procedure will resolve each dispute within one-hundred (100) calendar days...
>
> Selection of the Mediator. Prior to the contract award for the design work, an independent mediator free of conflict of interest and financial bias, shall be selected by mutual agreement of the owner, prime design professional [and other parties known to be involved at the inception of the project]. The parties shall share the mediator's fees and expenses in accordance with paragraph... In the event of failure to select a mediator under this process... an impartial group... shall appoint a mediator...

---

11 *ibid.*, pp. 229-230

Mandatory Mediation Procedure. ...any party, by written request to the mediator, [may] initiate mandatory mediation of any dispute...A request for mandatory mediation shall take precedence over and toll all other notice requirements for remedies concerning the same dispute ...

All documents, discussions, and other data developed during mediation shall remain confidential and not be disclosed by the mediator to any party not a party to the mediation.

In his own discretion, or on application of any Party, the mediator-arbitrator may include any other party to this agreement, by giving written notice to such other party.

All parties specifically acknowledge that the mediator, in his or her own discretion or upon the application of any party ..., may meet individually with any party while excluding other parties as determined within the discretion of the mediator.

Binding Arbitration. After failure to mediate a dispute, or failure of mediation to resolve a dispute, an aggrieved party shall request binding arbitration immediately upon refusal of a party to enter mediation or upon completion of a mediation without settlement of a dispute. The primary arbitrators shall be [   ]. He or she shall be other than the mediator described above."

Another modified form of med-arb is one where during the course of the mediation one party may ask the mediator to decide the remaining issues sitting as an arbitrator, provided the other parties concur. If any party objects, arbitration is conducted before a separate neutral. Proponents suggest it encourages the natural tendency of many parties in mediation to ask the mediator to resolve the intractable issues. It is unlikely, of course, that a disputant who has already done badly in caucus will feel comfortable authorising the mediator to arbitrate. However, the American Society of Forensic Engineers has adopted a standard clause for this type of dispute-resolution process, based on the Deep Foundations Construction Industry Roundtable's med-then-arb 100 day agreement. The key provision is:[12]

"Mediator's Decision. After failure of mediation to resolve a dispute, in full or at all, any disputant shall have the right to request the mediator to unilaterally decide all unresolved issues. The mediator and all other parties enjoined in the process shall then have three calendar days in which to accept or refuse this request. Acceptance must be unanimous.

Parties shall be bound by rules set forth hereinabove, for Mandatory Mediation, except that the mediator shall render a decision which shall be

---

12 *ibid.*, p. 231

binding upon the parties as those entered into of their own accord. The timetable given below shall apply."

There are two further major variants of med-arb. Advisory med-arb, where the arbitration award is non-binding, obviously has all the cost and time implications of any other similar process. It may be unsatisfactory for the parties merely to be left with the neutral's opinion of a likely outcome if the unresolved issues were to be settled by means of arbitration. Finally, under concilio-arbitration, which is a form of advisory med-arb, after attempting conciliation, the conciliator produces a draft award, setting out his opinion of the outcome if the dispute were fully litigated. Parties have an opportunity to respond, at which time they can highlight any manifest errors and present further arguments and evidence before the neutral makes a final award. If both parties accept the award, it becomes binding. If the award is rejected it has advisory status. If one party accepts the award and the matter subsequently proceeds to arbitration or litigation, the party rejecting the award may be obliged contractually to pay the whole of both parties' legal costs in the event that the same result is achieved in litigation.[13]

The Canadians have been innovative in facing the challenge of med-arb. David C Elliott[14] refers to the Institute of Law Research and Reform's proposals which recommended that to encourage settlement the arbitral tribunal should be able, with the consent of the parties, to use mediation and other ADR techniques at any stage of the arbitration without the arbitral tribunal being disqualified from changing from a facilitative to arbitral role as circumstances subsequently required. When passed, Alberta's Arbitration Act 1991 stated in section 35:

"(1) The members of an arbitral tribunal may, if the parties consent, use mediation, conciliation or similar techniques during the arbitration to encourage settlement of the matters in dispute.

(2) After the members of an arbitral tribunal use a technique referred to in subsection (1), they may resume their roles as arbitrators without disqualification."

Interestingly, Elliott poses the question whether the Alberta Statute[15] would preclude court intervention where a

---

13 *Concilio-Arbitration Handbook: Rules and Commentary,* Rowland Williams, Butterworths, 1986
14 *ibid.*, pp. 177-8
15 *ibid.*, p. 178

mediator/arbitrator engaged in private caucus sessions (an intrinsic element of mediation) with one or other of the parties. He refers to section 19 of the Alberta Act. This states, in terms not dissimilar to those found in section 33 of the Arbitration Act 1996:

> "(1) An arbitral tribunal shall treat the parties equally and fairly
>
> (2) Each party shall be given an opportunity to present a case and to respond to the other parties' cases."

However, the argument must remain that parties who have consciously espoused some form of med-arb cannot afterwards impugn the result and, by some means of estoppel, must have expressly waived (to the extent possible at law) strict legal principles. In New South Wales, parties can expressly exclude the rules of natural justice in a med-arb procedure.[16]

"SETTLEMENT OF DISPUTES OTHERWISE THAN BY ARBITRATION

Settlement of disputes otherwise than by arbitration

(1) Parties to an arbitration agreement:
  (a) may seek settlement of a dispute between them by mediation, conciliation or similar means; or
  (b) may authorise an arbitrator or umpire to act as a mediator, conciliator or other non-arbitral intermediary between them (whether or not involving a conference to be conducted by the arbitrator or umpire), whether before or after proceeding to arbitration, and whether or not continuing with the arbitration.

(2) Where:
  (a) an arbitrator or umpire acts as a mediator, conciliator or intermediary (with or without a conference) under sub-section (1); and
  (b) that action fails to produce a settlement of the dispute acceptable to the parties to the dispute, no objection shall be taken to the conduct by the arbitrator or umpire of the subsequent arbitration proceedings solely on the ground that the arbitrator or umpire had previously taken that action in relation to the dispute.

(3) Unless the parties otherwise agree in writing, an arbitrator or umpire is bound by the rules of natural justice when seeking a settlement under sub-section (1).

(4) Nothing in sub-section (3) affects the application of the rules of natural justice to an arbitrator or umpire in other circumstances.

---

16 s.27(3) Commercial Arbitration Amendment Act 1990, NSW

(5) The time appointed by or under this Act or fixed by an arbitration agreement or by an order under section 48 for doing any act or taking any proceeding in or in relation to an arbitration is not affected by any action taken by an arbitrator or umpire under sub-section (1).

(6) Nothing in sub-section (5) shall be construed as preventing the making of an application to the Court for the making of an order under section 48."

Although not expressly endorsing med-arb, the Arbitration Act 1996 may make its operation easier. The tribunal's powers under sections 34 and 46(1)(b) were considered earlier in this chapter. A major purpose of the Arbitration Act 1996 has been to reduce the courts' capacity to intervene in arbitration and overturn the decisions of arbitral tribunals. The main powers of the courts are found in section 24 (power of the court to remove an arbitrator) and challenges to awards on the basis of serious irregularity which has replaced the earlier doctrine of arbitral misconduct. Under section 24, the courts' powers are subservient to any vested in an arbitral institution which may have the capacity to intervene. An arbitrator may be removed because "...circumstances exist that give rise to justifiable doubts as to his impartiality" (s. 24(i)(a)).

On the face of it, an arbitrator could be open to attack on this ground if he has engaged in private caucus sessions with the parties. However, if they have agreed to him adopting this course of action, it would be strongly arguable that they are subsequently estopped from denying the arbitrator's ability to act in this manner. A clearer instance, where objection would be understandable, would be where the parties have agreed to med-arb, but without private caucus sessions, and the mediator/arbitrator canvasses the views of one of the parties without the consent of the other, or fails to give either party a right of reply (*i.e.* commits a breach of natural justice).

Turning to "*serious irregularity*", the phrase has replaced arbitral "*misconduct*", and is defined in section 68 (2). For present purposes, the most pertinent circumstance appears to be that set out in (a):

"failure by the tribunal to comply with Section 33 (general duty of tribunal)"

The purpose of section 68(2)(a) is obvious; section 33(1)(a) obliges the arbitral tribunal to act fairly and impartially. This reflects the rules of natural justice; an arbitrator is to be free from bias and parties must be given a fair opportunity to put their own case and answer that of the opponent. However, section 33 suggests the tribunal can place some restraints on the parties.

No arbitrator is going to embark upon med-arb without the clear consent of the parties. Therefore, a breach of section 33 is unlikely unless the arbitrator has misapplied powers vested in him by the parties. Perhaps by allowing the arbitrator to caucus at the mediation stage they are impliedly suggesting that his actions cannot be subsequently impugned for a lack of impartiality. Support for this contention can be found in section 73 of the 1996 Act. In common parlance, it states "you cannot have your cake and eat it". It prevents a party who takes part in an arbitration from delaying any objection to the arbitrator's jurisdiction. Key provisions for present purposes are:

- the proceedings have been improperly conducted; or
- there has been a failure to comply with the arbitration agreement or with any provision of Part 1 of the Act; or
- there has been any other irregularity affecting the arbitrator or the proceedings.

The aggrieved party now has to raise the objection when aware of the circumstance giving rise to the ground of objection or is otherwise prevented from mentioning the irregularity. Further, as well as other procedural hurdles, there is a general time limit under section 70(3) of the 1996 Act.

All in all, it seems unlikely that a consensual med-arb (how could it be anything different?) could be automatically questioned on the grounds of serious irregularity unless the mediator/arbitrator had so departed from the parties' prescribed process for the procedure as to render the process wholly different from the one to which they had consented. The conclusion is more tempting that an arbitrator in a med-arb would better rely on section 46(1)(b) and operate as an *amiable compositeur,* perhaps allied to an inquisitorial procedure under section 34(2)(g) of the 1996 Act with further reliance on section 34(2)(f). The provisions under section 46(1)(b) do not require the arbitrator to act in accordance with the law and thereby do not leave him open to attack under section 68 of the 1996 Act.

Lawyers in England and Wales, perhaps more conservative than those in other common law jurisdictions, do worry that med-arb clauses offend against the principles of natural justice. Unfortunately, many of the decided cases concerning natural justice relate either to civil liberties or are extremely old. In general, they sit unhappily with the aims of modern-day commercial arbitration and ignore the fact that commercial parties may at times be prepared to sacrifice some degree of legal and procedural subtlety in the interests of quicker and cheaper dispute resolution. That said, procedural safeguards can never be wholly disregarded. An arbitrator should approach his task with no preconceptions. For instance, the application of personal knowledge by an arbitrator can remove the capacity to listen attentively to the parties' own views, however misguided. He should allow the parties to address him further on the application of personal knowledge in case his views can be legitimately changed.

Ordinarily breaches of natural justice can be waived, although it has been suggested that certain irregularities may be so serious and fundamental in their effect as to amount *ipso facto* to a denial of justice and are beyond being waived.[17] However, if parties have a detailed med-arb clause a modern commercial court in England and Wales might have some difficulty in ignoring the express wishes of the parties.

It is easy for lawyers to overstate and exaggerate the difficulties of the med-arb process. Lawyers are in the generality by nature conservative and trained to be cautious. The value of med-arb lies in its supposed fault – there is likely to be an increasingly strong consumer demand for a neutral who can function effectively in both the mediation and subsequent arbitration phases of a dispute. Med-arb may assist a party who is in a weaker bargaining position at the mediation stage. A party with a strong case, but an inferior economic position, may feel obliged, having committed time and money to the mediation, to accept a less than adequate solution which could be bettered if he had the appropriate staying power. The mediator's capacity to change from a facilitative to an adjudicative function may help the weaker party by placing the neutral in a position where he has a more intimate knowledge of both parties' cases during the arbitral stage.

Even if the apparent legal difficulties are not fully resolved by this sleight, it may assist if the adjudicative stage is not subject either to the Arbitration Acts 1950–1979, or its replacement statute, the Arbitration Act 1996, and the adjudicative neutral sits as an expert.

There can be a fine dividing line between an adjudicative and an arbitral role. In the words of Ronald Bernstein QC:[18]

---

17 *Haigh* v *Haigh* (1861) 31 LJ Ch 420 per Turner LJ
18 *Handbook of Arbitration Practice*, Sweet & Maxwell, 1998, p. 19

"A contract may provide that disputes arising under it are to be resolved by some third person acting not as arbitrator but as an expert. ... The procedure involved is not arbitration ..."

Unfortunately the application of such a broad principle may be not as simple as that. According to Mustill and Boyd:[19]

"The way in which the reference is described in the agreement to refer is not conclusive as to the character of the proceedings. Thus, even an explicit agreement that a matter be dealt with by arbitration does not mean that the parties intended the proceedings to be the type of arbitration which is the subject of the Arbitration Acts or the common law of arbitration. For example, the use of this word is consistent with an intention to invoke a process which involves a decision by an impartial body, but not one which is binding in law."

Mustill and Boyd further comment:[20]

"... provisions purporting to exclude the Arbitration Acts, or providing that the tribunal shall sit as experts and not as Arbitrators could not be regarded as consistent with an intention to refer disputes to arbitration".

In one helpful case, *Sports Maska Inc.* v *Zittrer* [21], the Supreme Court of Canada considered the language used was not decisive. What may be described by the parties as an expert determination may, on objective analysis, be an arbitration. The distinction has now been considered in one English case, by His Honour Judge Humphrey LLoyd QC, *Cape Durasteel Ltd* v *Rosser* and *Russell Building Services Ltd* [22] who decided a clause described by the parties as an adjudication provision in fact committed them to arbitration.

Perhaps however the best solution is for those who advocate the greater use of the med-arb process to develop a coherent code of conduct for neutrals and the parties using them. By all means allow the neutral to use confidential information revealed to him, provided that it is specifically referred to in any award: impose a professional duty on the neutral to disqualify himself if he forms the view that for any reason it is not possible for him to act impartially because of the nature of the confidential information disclosed to him during the mediation phase (fraud, dishonesty, wrongdoing, *etc.*) and above all have clear guidelines as to when the mediation stage is to be deemed concluded and the arbitral phase to begin. Consider whether it is

---

19 *Commercial Arbitration* (2nd edn.), Butterworths, 1989, p. 49
20 *ibid.*, p. 109
21 (1988) 1 SCR 564
22 (1996) 46 Con LR 7523

appropriate for such a decision to be made by the neutral — whether it requires a joint decision of the parties, or simply the unilateral decision of one of the parties following a defined cooling off period of a specific number of days after the final mediation meeting.

Interestingly, although there is vehement opposition from some English lawyers to the whole idea of med-arb the same hostility is not found in other jurisdictions. Examples from Canada and Australia have already been discussed earlier in this chapter. For proponents of med-arb clauses some comfort may be drawn from overseas. For instance, Article 10 of the ICC Optional Rules of Conciliation does not preclude the appointment of a former conciliator as arbitrator of the same dispute. Alan Shilston[23] has written about the Bermuda International Conciliation and Arbitration Bill 1993 (since enacted), which contains important conciliation provisions. For purposes of interpretation conciliation in the Act includes mediation; and "Conciliation Rules" mean the UNCITRAL Conciliation Rules:

> "Where the parties have agreed in writing that a person appointed as a conciliator shall act as an arbitrator, in the event of the conciliation proceedings failing to produce a settlement acceptable to the parties no objection shall be taken to the appointment of such person as an arbitrator, or to his conduct of the arbitration proceedings or to any award, solely on the ground that he had acted previously as conciliator in connection with some or all of the matters referred to arbitration."

Similarly, in the same article Alan Shilston refers to a Hong Kong initiative[24] which permitted mediation to be followed by arbitration, should the parties expressly agree. A similar position also exists in Singapore.[25] Before discussing the position in Singapore, Shilston stated:

> "In some jurisdictions, for example Germany, the judges actively attempt to reconcile parties in civil proceedings. It is understood that caucusing does not take place unlike the US jurisdictions. In the Asian Pacific Rim regional cultural preferences in the matter of third party involvement in dispute settlement lean heavily in the direction of conciliation or mediation. European contractors are active in the region and as a matter of business, particularly the British, should be informed of background state law provisions that exist which allow the possibility of conciliation or mediation to blend with arbitration, should the parties so desire.

---

23 "Med-Arb, Can it Work?" (1994) 60, *JCI Arb 1*, pp.1-2
24 *ibid.*, p. 3
25 "The MED-ARB debate continued" (1995) *JCI Arb 2*, pp. 111, 112

Regional dispute resolution centres, such as Hong Kong, Bermuda and now Singapore, with Government as a facilitator through statutory enactments, provide settings wherein MED-ARB could take place."

Shilston then specifically sets out particular provisions of the Singapore International Arbitration Act 1994:

"Appointment of Conciliator

16.(1)   In any case where an agreement provides for the appointment of a conciliator by a person who is not one of the parties and that person refuses to make the appointment or does not make it within the time specified in the agreement or, if no time is so specified, within a reasonable time of being requested by any party to the agreement to make the appointment, the Chairman for the time being of the Singapore International Arbitration Centre may, on the application of any party to the agreement, appoint a conciliator who shall have the like powers to act in the conciliation proceedings as if he had been appointed in accordance with the terms of the agreement.

(2)   The Chief Justice may if he thinks fit, by notification published in the *Gazette*, appoint any other person to exercise the powers of the Chairman of the Singapore International Arbitration Centre under sub-section (1).

(3)   Where an arbitration agreement provides for the appointment of a conciliator and further provides that the person so appointed shall act as an arbitrator in the event of conciliation proceedings failing to produce a settlement acceptable to the parties -

(a)   No objection shall be taken to the appointment of such person as an arbitrator, or to his conduct of the arbitral proceedings, solely on the ground that he had acted previously as a conciliator in connection with some or all of the matters referred to arbitration;

(b)   If such person declines to act as an arbitrator, any other person appointed as an arbitrator shall not be required first to act as a conciliator unless a contrary intention appears in the arbitration agreement.

(4)   Unless a contrary intention appears therein, an agreement which provides for the appointment of a conciliator shall be deemed to contain a provision that in the event of the conciliation proceedings failing to produce a settlement acceptable to the parties within 4 months, or such longer period as the parties may agree to, of the date of the appointment of the conciliator or, where he is appointed by name in the agreement, of the receipt by him of written notification of the existence of a dispute, the conciliation proceedings shall thereupon terminate.

Power of Arbitrator to act as Conciliator

17.(1) If all parties to any arbitral proceedings consent in writing and for so long as no party has withdrawn his consent in writing, an arbitrator or umpire may act as a conciliator.

   (2) An arbitrator or umpire acting as conciliator -
      (a) may communicate with the parties to the arbitral proceedings collectively or separately; and
      (b) shall treat information obtained by him from a party to the arbitral proceedings as confidential, unless that party otherwise agrees or unless sub-section (3) applies.

   (3) Where confidential information is obtained by an arbitrator or umpire from a party to the arbitral proceedings during conciliation proceedings and those proceedings terminate without the parties reaching agreement in settlement of their dispute, the arbitrator or umpire shall before resuming the arbitral proceedings disclose to all other parties to the arbitral proceedings as much of that information as he considers material to the arbitral proceedings.

   (4) No objection shall be taken to the conduct of arbitral proceedings by a person solely on the ground that that person had acted previously as a conciliator in accordance with this section."

Traditionally, Hong Kong did not deviate from the English model. Statutory control of Hong Kong arbitration, found in the 1963 Arbitration Ordinance, was identical to the Arbitration Act 1950. Hong Kong enacted a new arbitration ordinance in 1982[26] which, although modelled on the Arbitration Act 1975, was significantly different. One of the principal differences from English practice was specific recognition of conciliation.

What was significant about the 1982 Arbitration Ordinance was its radicalism. The provisions relating to conciliation were set out in the following terms:

"2.   The principal Ordinance is amended by adding, after Part 1, the following Part-

Part A

CONCILIATION

Appointment of Conciliator.

2A. (1) In any case where an arbitration agreement provides for the appointment of a conciliator by a person who is not one of the

---

26 Arbitration (Amendment) Ord. No. 10/82

parties and that person refuses to make the appointment or does not make it within the time specified in the agreement or, if no time is so specified, within a reasonable time not exceeding 2 months of being informed of the existence of the dispute, any party to the agreement may serve the person in question with a written notice to appoint a conciliator (and shall forthwith serve a copy of the notice on the other parties to the agreement) and if the appointment is not made within 7 clear days after service of the notice the Court or a judge thereof may, on the application of any party to the agreement, appoint a conciliator who shall have the like powers to act in the conciliation proceedings as if he had been appointed in accordance with the terms of the agreement

(2) Where an arbitration agreement provides for the appointment of a conciliator and further provides that the person so appointed shall act as an arbitrator in the event of the conciliation proceedings failing to produce a settlement acceptable to the parties -

    (a) no objection shall be taken to the appointment of such person as an arbitrator, or to his conduct of the arbitration proceedings, solely on the ground that he had acted previously as a conciliator in connection with some or all of the matters referred to arbitration;

    (b) if such person declines to act as an arbitrator any other person appointed as an arbitrator shall not be required first to act as a conciliator unless a contrary intention appears in the arbitration agreement.

(3) Unless a contrary intention appears therein, an arbitration agreement which provides for the appointment of a conciliator shall be deemed to contain a provision that in the event of the conciliation proceedings failing to produce a settlement acceptable to the parties within 3 months, or such longer period as the parties may agree to, of the date of the appointment of the conciliator or, where he is appointed by name in the arbitration agreement, of the receipt by him of written notification of the existence of a dispute the proceedings shall thereupon terminate.

(4) If the parties to an arbitration agreement which provides for the appointment of a conciliator reach agreement in settlement of their differences and sign an agreement containing the terms of settlement (hereinafter referred to as the "settlement agreement") the settlement agreement shall, for the purposes of its enforcement, be treated as an award on an arbitration agreement and may, by leave of the Court or a judge thereof, be enforced in the same manner as a judgement or order to the same effect, and where leave is so given, may be entered in terms of the agreement."

The provisions set out above contained a number of significant features which are not even contemplated for inclusion in English law and practice. First, a recalcitrant party could be obliged to conciliate; the court had a statutory right and power to uphold conciliation agreements. Second, the Ordinance endorsed the principle of med-arb. Third, a finite period was set for completion of the conciliation phase. Fourth, statute maintained that any settlement agreement should, for the purposes of enforcement, have the same status as an arbitration award and be enforceable through the courts.

The matter of conciliation was considered further by the Law Reform Commission of Hong Kong[27] and its recommendations included in the Arbitration Ordinance in 1989. The relevant changes are set out below. Section 2A(1) was amended, section 2A(4) repealed and new sections 2B and 2C inserted.

"Appointment of Conciliator

2A.(1) In any case where an arbitration agreement provides for the appointment of a conciliator by a person who is not one of the parties and that person refuses to make the appointment or does not make it within the time specified in the agreement or, if no time is so specified, within a reasonable time of being requested by any party to the agreement to make the appointment, the Court or a judge thereof may, on the application of any party to the agreement, appoint a conciliator who shall have the like powers to act in the conciliation proceedings as if he had been appointed in accordance with the terms of the agreement.[Amendment 64 of 1989 s.4]

Power of arbitrator to act as conciliator

2B.(1) If all parties to a reference consent in writing, and for so long as no party withdraws in writing his consent, an arbitrator or umpire may act as a conciliator.

(2) An arbitrator or umpire acting as conciliator:
   (a) may communicate with the parties to the reference collectively or separately;
   (b) shall treat information obtained by him from a party to the reference as confidential, unless that party otherwise agrees or unless subsection (3) applies.

(3) Where confidential information is obtained by an arbitrator or umpire from a party to the reference during conciliation

---

27 Report on Commercial Arbitration

proceedings and those proceedings terminate without the parties reaching agreement in settlement of their dispute, the arbitrator or umpire shall, before resuming the arbitration proceedings, disclose to all other parties to the reference as much of that information as he considers is material to the arbitration proceedings.

(4) No objection shall be taken to the conduct of arbitration proceedings by an arbitrator or umpire solely on the ground that he had acted previously as arbitrator in accordance with this section. [Amendment 64 of 1989 s.5]

Settlement agreements

2C. If the parties to an arbitration agreement reach agreement in settlement of their dispute and enter into an agreement in writing containing the terms of settlement (the "settlement agreement") the settlement agreement shall, for the purposes of its enforcement, be treated as an award on an arbitration agreement and may, by leave of the Court or a judge thereof, be enforced in the same manner as a judgment or order to the same effect and, where leave is so given, judgment may be entered in terms of the agreement. [Amendment 64 of 1989 s.5]"

Outside the Far East and the world of construction law David C. Elliott[28] highlights examples of non-construction related med-arb provisions including ones from the World Intellectual Property Organisation:

"(a) The mediator shall promote the settlement of the issues in dispute between the parties in any manner that the mediator believes to be appropriate, but shall have no authority to impose a settlement on the parties.

(b) Where the mediator believes that any issues in dispute between the parties are not susceptible to resolution through mediation, the mediator may propose, for the consideration of the parties, procedures or means for resolving those issues which the mediator considers are most likely, having regard to the circumstances of the dispute and any business relationship between the parties, to lead to the most efficient, least costly and most productive settlement of those issues. In particular, the mediator may so propose:
(i) an expert determination of one or more particular issues;
(ii) arbitration;
(iii) the submission of last offers of settlement by each party and, in the absence of a settlement through mediation, arbitration conducted on the basis of those last offers pursuant to an arbitral procedure in which the mission of the arbitral

---

28 op.cit. n. at p.13, 180

tribunal is confined to determining which of the last offers shall prevail; or

(iv) arbitration in which the mediator will, with the express consent of the parties, act as a sole arbitrator, it being understood that the mediator may, in the arbitral proceedings, take into account information received during the mediation."

WIPO recommends the following clause for a med-arb process:

"Any dispute, controversy or claim arising under, out of or relating to this contract and any subsequent amendments of this contract, including, without limitation, its formation, validity, binding effect, interpretation, performance, breach or termination, as well as non-contractual claims, shall be submitted to mediation in accordance with the WIPO Mediation Rules. The place of mediation shall be.... . The language to be used in the mediation shall be.... .

If, and to the extent that, any such dispute, controversy or claim has not been settled pursuant to the mediation within [60][90] days of the commencement of mediation, it shall, upon the filing of a Request for Arbitration by either party, be referred to and finally determined by arbitration in accordance with the WIPO Arbitration Rules. Alternatively, if, before the expiration of the said period of [60][90] days, either party fails to participate or to continue to participate in the mediation, the dispute, controversy or claim shall, upon the filing of a Request for Arbitration by the other party, be referred to and finally determined by arbitration in accordance with the WIPO Arbitration Rules. The arbitral tribunal shall consist of [three arbitrators] [a sole arbitrator]. The place of arbitration shall be ... . The language to be used in the arbitral proceedings shall be ... . The dispute, controversy or claim referred to arbitration shall be decided in accordance with the law of ... ."

If med-arb and related techniques are to make inroads in the United Kingdom (the progress of 'straight' mediation being rather slow), much will depend on international trade disputes introducing national companies to the benefits of a system which could potentially bring the best of both worlds, putting certainty into the mediation process when negotiations fail on some or all of the issues.

Chapter 5

Legal Concerns

Limitation Periods

Whenever a would-be plaintiff is considering how best to resolve his dispute, both he and his lawyers must remember the importance of the limitation periods. If a claim is to be litigated through the courts or through arbitration that claim must ordinarily be commenced within the statutory period of limitation. The requirement to assert the relevance of the limitation period is the defendant's; the question of limitation may serve as part of his defence to the claim. The Limitation Act 1980 is the primary source of the law on limitation of actions. This provides:

- an action arising out of a simple contract must be brought within six years of the date when the cause of action accrued (*i.e.* the date the breach occurred) (s.5); and
- any claim under a contract executed as a deed must be brought within 12 years of the date on which the cause of action accrued (s.8).

The trigger date is the date when the breach of contract occurred. This can be difficult to assess; particularly in construction claims. If, for instance, the claim is based on defective work it may be extremely difficult to ascertain the date on which particular work was carried out. Therefore, construction contracts often assume that the date of breach is the date of practical or substantial completion (when all the work has been carried out and, minor defects excepted, the client has beneficial use). That does not exclude other possible dates. For instance, if the contractor fails to carry out an instruction to make good defects, that may well constitute a further breach of contract on his part. Indeed, the contractor will not finally discharge his obligations until the end of the defects liability or maintenance period. He may therefore be liable for the whole of that period. A further complication in fixing limitation periods results from section 32 Limitation Act 1980. This deals with deliberate concealment on the part of the defendant. The commencement of the limitation period is, in such circumstances, suspended until such time as the plaintiff has either discovered the concealment or is in a position where he could, with reasonable diligence, have discovered it.

Many claims brought are argued by lawyers both as breaches of contract on the part of the defendant and, in the alternative, as giving rise to causes of action in tort. For a time it was suggested that a plaintiff who had a detailed contract with the defendant could not at the same time assert rights against the defendant in the law of negligence[1]. However, the courts have recently reasserted with some vigour that the existence of a formal contract does not necessarily preclude the existence of concurrent rights in negligence which may, on occasions, be more extensive[2]. Obviously, a plaintiff cannot obtain double recovery, however his claim is argued.

The Limitation Act 1980 affects negligence claims quite differently from contract ones. Section 2 Limitation Act 1980 provides that no action founded on tort can be brought more than six years from the date on which the cause of action accrued. This is the date when damage was suffered. This may be long after the date on which a breach of contract occurred. This means the plaintiff has potentially a longer time period in which to bring his claim. The fact that a cause of action in tort arises when damage occurs is a possible source of injustice to plaintiffs. There could be circumstances in which a plaintiff, through no fault of his own, was unaware that he had in fact suffered damage. The House of Lords decision in *Pirelli General Cable Works Ltd* v *Oscar Faber & Partners*[3] is a notorious example of this. Oscar Faber, a well-known firm of consulting engineers, designed a chimney stack which was built in 1969. According to expert evidence, cracks developed near the top of the chimney not later than 1970, which would not have been noticed on general routine maintenance. The damage was not discovered until 1977 and a Writ was issued in 1978. The House of Lords, whilst recognising what was at the time the unsatisfactory state of the law, held that the plaintiff's cause of action in tort arose in 1970 and was therefore clearly statute barred. The consequence of the Pirelli decision was that Parliament enacted the Latent Damage Act 1986. This Act

---

1 *Tai Hing Cotton Mill Ltd* v *Liu Chong Hing Bank Ltd* [1986] AC 80 (PC)

2 *Lancashire & Cheshire Associations of Baptist Churches Inc.* v *Howard & Seddon Partnership* [1993] 3 AER 467; *Conway* v *Crowe Kelsey Partner & Another (1994)* CILL 927; *Wessex Regional Health Authority* v *HLM Design Limited (1993)* CILL 907; *Holt and Another* v *Payne Skillington (a Firm) and Another*, The Times, 22nd December 1995 (CA)

3 [1983] 2 AC 1

introduced new sections 14A and 14B into the Limitation Act 1980. These were a material change to the old law. They allowed a plaintiff, who had not commenced proceedings within six years of incurring damage, to commence proceedings within a further three-year period from the date on which he first became aware that he had incurred damage, if his failure to become aware of the damage within the primary six year period was reasonable. Similar principles apply in regard to personal injury claims. In addition, to bring some certainty to the defendant's position, parliament also created a long-stop period of 15 years, effectively extinguishing the plaintiff's right to claim, calculated from the date of the last alleged act of negligence on the part of the defendant.

The importance of recognising statutory limitation periods cannot be overstated. No defendant is going helpfully to draw a would-be claimant's attention to the need to bring his claim in court or arbitration before it becomes statute barred. Such considerations become all the more critical when discussing ADR solutions. No claimant can afford to become so embroiled in the ADR process as to ignore the time when issue of a protective writ to avoid a particular claim becoming statute barred may become essential, rather than simply prudent. Conversely, it might benefit a cynical defendant to go through the motions of seeking an ADR solution with a particular claimant but with no intention of taking the process seriously; simply using it as a stalling tactic in the hope that the claim will either go away through inertia on the part of the claimant or, as an attractive alternative, subsequently be found to be statute barred.

A further complication under certain construction contracts is the existence of a distinctive dispute-resolution mechanism which needs to be followed. Leaving to one side non mandatory statutory adjudication under the Housing Grants Construction and Regeneration Act 1996 which affects a broad range of construction contracts and which provides an additional option for the resolution of disputes, an obvious example is found in the ICE Conditions of Contract 6th Edition. Clause 66, the relevant clause under both ICE 5th Edition and 6th Edition (the principal standard-form civil engineering contract) for the resolution of disputes, requires an engineer's decision as a condition precedent to any subsequent arbitration. A major distinction between the 5th and 6th Editions was that under the latter the parties could choose whether a dispute should be referred to a conciliator or should proceed direct to arbitration.

Similarly, the principal building contract, JCT 80, which has the option of non mandatory adjudication, needs to be treated with caution. Problems can be caused by the so-called Final Certificate which limits the time period for commencing arbitration or litigation.

Although there was a general power under section 27 Arbitration Act 1950 (rather more narrowly drawn in section 12 Arbitration Act 1996) for the High Court to extend the period during which arbitration proceedings may be commenced (to avoid undue hardship to a claimant) it has been unreliable to rely on the exercise of the discretion in construction cases although its use has not been unknown in maritime disputes. There are two building cases on the point and a civil engineering one. The building cases both relate to JCT 80. In the first, *McLaughlin & Harvey* v *P & O Developments Ltd*,[4] the Commercial Court held that the period during which arbitration proceedings could be commenced in regard to a Final Certificate could be extended by the court under section 27 Arbitration Act 1950. In the more recent case, *Crown Estate Commissioners* v *John Mowlem & Co Ltd*[5] the Court of Appeal held that the decision in *McLaughlin & Harvey* was incorrect and that there was no discretionary power under section 27 Arbitration Act 1950 to extend the period during which arbitration proceedings could be commenced. The latter decision does not sit happily with *Christiani and Nielsen Ltd* v *Birmingham City Council*.[6] In this case two issues were before His Honour Judge Hicks QC, one of which was: could the three-month period to commence arbitration proceedings under Clause 66(3)(a) be extended under section 27 Arbitration Act 1950?

For reasons relating to the particular case before him, the judge was not obliged to consider the issue in detail. However, he indicated that he would have approved a section 27 extension if necessary.

Maritime cases have traditionally been flexible. In *Liberian Shipping Corporation ("Pegasus")* v *A. King & Sons Ltd*,[7] the Court of Appeal was generous in its interpretation of "undue hardship". A charterparty included the clause:

> "[A]ny claim must be made in writing and claimant's arbitrator appointed within 3 months of final discharge, and where this provision is not complied with, the claim should be deemed to be waived and absolutely barred."

4 (1991) 28 Con. LR 15
5 (1994) CILL 986
6 (1995) CILL 1014
7 [1967] 2 QB 86

During the charter a number of delays and disasters occurred including a fire by spontaneous combustion of the cargo. Finally, discharge was completed on 26th March 1966. Over the next three months the parties debated their respective claims although the three-month period expired without settlement being achieved. About ten days later the owners, whose claim for damage to the vessel exceeded £30,000, applied under section 27 Arbitration Act 1950 for an extension of time. The Court of Appeal held, by a majority, that the owners should be permitted an extension of 14 days from the date of the Court's judgment. In the words of Salmon LJ:[8]

> "I cannot find anything in section 27 which in these circumstances compels me to say that it would not impose undue hardship on the claimants to hold they must forfeit their claim to some £33,000 because of this small delay which has had no effect at all on the respondents. ... I have no doubt at all that if two ordinary business men entering into this contract had been asked if it would cause undue hardship to refuse to extend the time should circumstances such as the present occur, they would both unhesitatingly have answered 'yes'. I am not prepared to hold that the court's powers under the section should be very rarely exercised. Still less that they should be exercised freely. The question as to whether or not those powers should be exercised must turn exclusively on the particular facts of each case in which the question arises."

Two of the more notable applications of the *"Pegasus"* are the judgment of Brandon J in *Moscow V/O Export Exportkhleb* v *Helmville Ltd (The "Jocelyne")*[9] and the judgment of the Court of Appeal in *Libra Shipping & Trading Corporation Ltd* v *Northern Sales Ltd (The "Aspen Trader")*[10]

In the *"Jocelyne"*, Brandon J, after careful consideration of the relevant circumstances, concluded that the case was not one where the court should extend the plaintiff's time for bringing arbitration proceedings on the grounds of "undue hardship" within the meaning of section 27 Arbitration Act 1950. There had been a very long delay with some two years of that attributable to delays on the part of the plaintiff. These had seriously prejudiced the defendant. Brandon J set down a number of guidelines for use in section 27 Arbitration Act 1950 applications:[11]

---

8   at 107
9   [1977] 2 Lloyd's LR 121
10 [1981] 1 Lloyd's LR 273
11 at 129

- The words "undue hardship" in section 27 should not be construed too narrowly.
- Undue hardship means excessive hardship and, where the hardship is due to the fault of the claimant, it means hardship the consequences of which are out of proportion to such other fault.
- In deciding whether to extend time or not, the court should look at all the relevant circumstances of a particular case.
- In particular, the court should consider the following:
  - the length of the delay
  - the amount at stake
  - whether the delay was due to the fault of the claimant or to circumstances outside his control
  - if it was due to the fault of the claimant, the degree of fault
  - whether the claimant was misled by the other party
  - whether the other party has been prejudiced by the delay, and, if so, the degree of such   prejudice.

In "The Aspen Trader", Lloyd J refused to grant an extension of time under section 27 Arbitration Act 1950 in a demurrage dispute. In reversing the decision of the Commercial Court, Brandon LJ stated:[12]

> "To lose the chance of prosecuting a claim for $300,000 because of some neglect or inefficiency in a firm's office does seem to me to be grave hardship. If the delay has caused no problems to the other side, then it seems to me that to shut a claimant out from such a claim would involve undue hardship within the meaning of that expression in s.27 of the Arbitration Act, 1950."

More recently, in *International Petroleum Refining and Supply SDAD Ltd v Elpis Finance SA (The "Faith")*,[13] Hobhouse J considered whether an application for an extension of time for leave to appeal should be granted. A party who wished to reserve his right to take a matter to court either by way of appeal or by way of remission had to ensure that the award was taken up in time to enable that application to be made. Where parties voluntarily allowed the time-limit to expire by a substantial amount a party should not be allowed later to challenge the finality of an award other than in very exceptional circumstances. The rather narrower grounds under section 12 Arbitration Act 1996 were considered in

---

12 at 280
13 [1993] 2 Lloyd's LR 408

Fox and another v *Guram*, unreported, Commercial Court, 3rd October 1997 and offered little or no hope to a party seeking to extend time, a trend reflected in other Commercial Court cases.[14]

Achieving Certainty in the ADR Process

One of the constant criticisms made of ADR and a possible benefit brought by med-arb is that, even if successful, any agreement is difficult to enforce legally if a party later reneges. Some certainty is possible if, following a successful mediation, the parties set out the terms of their settlement in writing and in a form which is enforceable in the courts without further analysis of the issues. Here, lawyers can be of assistance. First, although there has not been a judgment of the courts, the agreement can be written so as to be an enforceable agreement which, if necessary, the courts can be asked to enforce. Such agreements can be based on a Tomlin Order, named after Tomlin J. In a *Practice Note*[15] he said that where terms of compromise were agreed with the intention that an action in the courts would be stayed in accordance with the terms scheduled to the Order, the Order should be worded as follows:

> "And, the plaintiff and the defendant having agreed to the terms set forth in the schedule hereto, it is ordered that all further proceedings in this action be stayed, except for the purpose of carrying such terms into effect. Liberty to apply as to carrying such terms into effect."

In litigation, if the agreed terms are breached, enforcement requires first that the action is restored under the "liberty to apply" provision with an order then obtained to compel compliance. Second, if that order is itself breached, enforcement is then possible in court. If an ADR settlement has occurred, following the earlier issue of a writ, an unamended Tomlin Order is applicable. If there has been no prior or concurrent litigation, the parties will need to produce a specially drafted agreement which includes the following:

- the identity of the parties;
- recitals indicating that various disputes have arisen, the disputes have been referred to mediation by... and that settlement has now been achieved in the terms set out below;

---

14 *Cathiship SA* v *Allanasons Ltd (the Catherine Hoken)* [1998] 3 AER 714; *Grimaldi Compagnia di Navigazione SpA* v *Sekihyo Line Ltd* [1998] 3 AER 943
15 [1927 WN 290]

- the terms of settlement;
- a provision to the effect that the agreement shall be deemed to have as between the parties the same effect as if the agreement had been reached as a result of or during the course of litigation and that any party finding another party to be in breach of the terms of the agreement is at liberty to apply to a nominated court for necessary orders to ensure compliance by the recalcitrant party with the terms of the agreement.

A second method to assist enforcement is to state that the agreement shall be deemed to have the same effect as an arbitration award to which the Arbitration Act 1996 applies. Then, if necessary, enforcement of the "award" can be made through section 66 Arbitration Act 1996 in the courts.

Privilege and Witness Compellability

The doctrines of privilege and witness compellability may cause considerable problems in the context of ADR. Difficulties are not assisted by the lack of direct judicial guidance. Questions include:

- If a mediation fails and the parties return to the courts or to arbitration, what is the status of documentation prepared and tendered for the purposes of the failed mediation? Is it safe from disclosure in subsequent court or arbitration proceedings?
- Is the mediator at risk of being called to give evidence in subsequent court or arbitration proceedings on behalf of either one or other of the parties?
- Can the mediator remain silent concerning comments made to him during the private caucus sessions?
- Whether the mediation is successful or not, what happens if there is subsequent related litigation and one or other of the parties considers what happened in the previous mediation to be relevant and either seeks specific discovery of mediation documents or attempts to require the attendance of participants in the mediation at the subsequent litigation?

Although parties often state expressly that non-binding mediation is to be carried out between them on a without prejudice basis, even if the process is not expressly stated to be without prejudice it would probably be treated as such by lawyers. Non-binding mediation has much in common with ordinary settlement talks that parties to litigation might attempt. The phrase "without prejudice" simply means that if settlement talks are unsuccessful, any statements made will be privileged; no reference can be made to them in any subsequent litigation or arbitration proceedings. In *Rush & Tompkins Ltd* v *Greater London Council*,[16] Lord Griffiths said:

> "The rule applies to exclude all negotiations genuinely aimed at settlement whether oral or in writing from being given in evidence. A competent solicitor will always head any negotiating correspondence 'without prejudice' to make it clear beyond doubt that in the event of the negotiations being unsuccessful they are not to be referred to at the subsequent trial. However, the application of the rule is not dependent upon the use of the phrase 'without prejudice' and if it is clear from the surrounding circumstances that the parties were seeking to compromise the action, evidence of the content of those negotiations will, as a general rule, not be admissible at the trial and cannot be used to establish an admission or partial admission."

The privilege in statements made on a without prejudice basis is the joint one of the parties and extends to their solicitors.[17] It can only be waived with the consent of each of the parties.

Some assistance can be drawn from matrimonial cases which may be subject to conciliation. If negotiations have taken place in the presence of a mediator or a counsellor, with offers and suggestions being relayed to the parties via the neutral, those negotiations are privileged. They have the same protection as if made in correspondence. In a relatively old case, *McTaggart* v *McTaggart*[18] an interview had been arranged between spouses in front of a probation officer on a without prejudice basis. The Court of Appeal held that either spouse was entitled to object to evidence of what had been said being admitted at a subsequent trial. However, as the privilege was that of the parties, the probation officer was not able to object if the parties then chose to waive the privilege in the statements made before the probation officer. The judge was bound to admit them as evidence at trial. The modern law, at least in the context of matrimonial proceedings, was stated in *D* v *NSPCC*:[19]

---

16 [1989] AC 1280 at 1299
17 *La Roche* v *Armstrong* [1922] 1 KB 485
18 [1949] P 94, at 96 per Cohen LJ
19 [1978] AC 171, at 236–237 per Lord Simon

"With increasingly facile divorce and the vast rise in the number of broken marriages, with their concomitant penury and demoralisation, it came to be realized, in the words of Buckmill LJ in *Mole v Mole at p.33*: 'in matrimonial disputes the state is also an interested party, it is more interested in reconciliation than in divorce'. This was the public interest that led to the application by analogy of the privilege of 'without prejudice' communications to cover communications made in the course of matrimonial conciliation (see *McTaggart v McTaggart; Mole v Mole; Theodoropoulas v Theodoropoulas*) so indubitably an extension of the law that the text books treat it as a separate category of relevant evidence which may be withheld from the court. It cannot be classified, like traditional 'without prejudice' communications, as a 'privilege in aid of litigation...'."

A situation could arise in mediation akin to that in *Rush & Tompkins v Greater London Council*. The plaintiff brought an action against two defendants but eventually settled with the first defendant. The second defendant sought disclosure of the without prejudice negotiations between the plaintiff and the first defendant which were obviously relevant to the action between the plaintiff and the second defendant. In reversing the decision of the Court of Appeal, and upholding that of the first instance judge, the House of Lords held that the provisional without prejudice negotiations between the plaintiff and the first defendant were subject to privilege. According to Lord Griffiths, a view concurred in by the other members of the House of Lords, it was untenable to suggest that once negotiations were successful privilege in the without prejudice correspondence had served its purpose and must be disregarded.

The question of privilege, arising out of a mediation hearing has been addressed in the United States and Australia. In the United States the Southern District Court of New York has ruled that documents from an ADR proceeding are protected from discovery and subsequent court proceedings under the attorney–client privilege and work product doctrine. This ruling was made in the case of *North River Insurance Co. v Columbia Casualty Co.*[20] North River claimed losses incurred for asbestos-related defence costs under an insurance policy with Owens-Corning Fiberglass. Following an ADR procedure between North River and Owens-Corning, North River was required to pay Owens-Corning's defence costs. North River then sued a number of reinsurers, including Columbia Casualty, to

---

20 *Dispute Resolution Times*, New York, June 1995

recover part of the defence costs. Columbia Casualty argued that such costs were not covered under the original policy between North River and Owens-Corning and were therefore not subject to the reinsurance agreement. Columbia Casualty requested discovery of all of North River's documents relating to its dispute with Owens-Corning. North River requested a protective order from the Southern District Court on the grounds that documents disclosed in the context of an ADR procedure were protected from discovery under the attorney–client privilege and work product doctrine. The court found that Columbia Casualty and North River were not represented by the same counsel, did not share legal expenses, did not pursue a co-ordinated litigation strategy and therefore lacked a common interest. In April 1996[21] the American state of Pennsylvania brought into effect a law granting statutory privilege to most communications resulting from mediation:

> "disclosure of mediation communications and mediation documents may not be required or compelled through discovery or any other process. Mediation communications and mediation documents should not be admissible in any action or proceeding, including, but not limited to, a judicial, administrative or arbitration action or proceeding."

By this law, Pennsylvania aims to encourage mediation and to avoid any risks that the court may subpoena parties or mediators to obtain documents and information. The statutory exemptions are:

- Settlement documents which may be introduced in an action to enforce settlement.
- Any communication or conduct that is relevant evidence in a criminal action.
- Fraudulent communications made during mediations which become relevant evidence in an action to enforce or set aside a mediated agreement as a result of fraud.

In Australia, the confidentiality of the mediation process was considered in the long running proceedings in *AWA Ltd* v *Daniels & Others*.[22]

At an interlocutory stage, Rolfe J sitting in the Supreme Court of New South Wales, was called upon to decide whether or not information disclosed by one of the parties during an aborted mediation could later be used by one of the other parties. One of the

---

21 *Dispute Resolution Times*, New York, Spring 1996
22 Unrep., 2 May 1992

defendants had issued a Notice to Produce requiring production of documents, the existence of which had been disclosed in the course of the mediation between the parties.

The court refused to set aside the Notice to Produce, allowing the defendant to utilise facts obtained during the mediation. Rolfe J drew a close analogy between mediation and settlement negotiations and relied on the decision of the High Court in *Field* v *Commissioner of Railways (NSW)*[23] which narrowed the privilege pertaining to settlement negotiations such that it did not preclude a party leading evidence on facts ascertained during the negotiations.

Later, in the same case, and in the context of an objection to the tender of the same documents, Rogers CJ overruled the objection but said:

> "It is of the essence of successful mediation that parties should be able to reveal all relevant matters without an apprehension that the disclosure may subsequently be used against them ... were the position otherwise, unscrupulous parties could use and abuse the mediation process by treating it as a gigantic, penalty free discovery process ..."

One relevant factor in both judges' decisions appears to have been that the defendant's solicitor was aware of the possible existence of the material sought before the mediation and that the documents were probably discoverable if their relevance could be established. Nonetheless, it appears unsafe to assume, at least in Australia, that parties cannot utilise information obtained through mediation in subsequent court proceedings. The issue does not appear to have subsequently come before the courts, although many commentators predict legislative intervention.[24]

In order to protect mediators from the risk of becoming involved in any subsequent litigation or arbitration proceedings, most mediation rules provide that an appointed mediator, who is under contract to the parties, is expressly precluded from being called to give evidence in any subsequent litigation or arbitration. In any event, most mediators take practical measures under their own appointments to ensure that they reduce the possibility of being subjected to document subpoenas or any other court process. More often than not the parties will agree that any documents prepared for and in the course of mediation, including the mediator's notes, will be destroyed at the termination of the proceedings.

---

23 (1957) 99 CLR 285
24 See Boulle, case note on *AWA Ltd* v *Daniels*, Vol.3 *Arbitration and Dispute Resolution Journal* 272 at 275

Enforceability of Mediation Clauses

Whenever parties embark upon non-binding mediation they understand that the procedure does not necessarily mean a successful outcome. It is a trite principle of English law (unlike the position in both the United States of America and Canada) that an agreement to enter into negotiations is unenforceable. For instance, Lord Denning MR stated in *Courtney and Fairburn Ltd v Tolaini Brothers (Hotels) Ltd* that such agreements were "too uncertain to have any binding force"[25]. Australia too has, on occasions, adopted the English approach: *Coal Cliff Collieries Pty Ltd v Sijehama Ltd* [26] although the Australian discussion of the enforceability of mediation clauses is more extended than that one decision and of some interest. So what happens if one of the parties decides not to play ball having entered a contract which requires ADR as the first tier of dispute resolution?

Some Australian courts have supported mediation clauses. In *Hooper Bailie Associated Ltd v Natcom Group Pty Ltd* [27] both parties to a construction dispute had agreed to conciliation in order to accelerate resolution of their dispute. The Supreme Court of New South Wales held, inter alia, that as the parties had agreed to conciliate, the court had power to order a stay of arbitration until the conclusion of the conciliation procedure. A similar result was achieved in *Elizabeth Bay Developments Pty Ltd v Boral Building Services Pty Ltd* [28] although on the facts of the case the particular mediation agreement was unenforceable because it lacked certainty. In one case, the Queensland Supreme Court (Master Horton) displayed greater conservatism and refused an application to stay litigation commenced in contravention of a conciliation clause, that case being *Allco Steel (Queensland) Pty Ltd v Torres Strait Gold Pty Ltd*:[29]

> "...[the contract] merely provides an agreement to conciliate [as distinct from one to litigate] and as such is severable from the binding agreement in which it is located. In other words, notwithstanding what I perceive to be a clear breach of the obligations to conciliate on the part of the plaintiff, the doctrine that the jurisdiction of the court cannot be ousted dominates any other principle that would require the plaintiff to honour its contractual obligations.

25 [1975] 1 WLR 297, at 301–2
26 (1992) 24 NSWLR 1
27 (1992) 28 NSWLR 194
28 Unrep., 28th March 1995
29 Unrep., 12th March 1990

An appeal was made to the inherent jurisdiction of the court to grant a stay, the condition precedent to the accruing of a cause of action not having been met, namely bona fide conciliation. In my view even if such relief was open, this discretionary relief must be refused as it is abundantly clear that the parties have taken up positions which effectively rule out compromise and conciliation..."

In a later case, *AWA Ltd v Daniels and Others*,[30] the Supreme Court of New South Wales expressly disapproved *Allco Steel*. Rogers J considered that the commencement of formal litigation without complying with the contractual provisions for mediation was an abuse of the process.

Similarly, the United States courts have upheld ADR clauses, where part of the contract between the parties, as a necessary first step prior to any litigation or arbitration. For instance, the District Court of Oregon specifically approved the earlier decision in *Southland Corporation v Keating* [31] in *Haertl Wolff Parker Inc. v Howard S. Wright Construction Co.*[32] to the effect:

"A contract providing for alternative dispute resolution should be enforced and one party should not be allowed to evade the contract and resort prematurely to the Courts"[33].

In what some commentators considered to be a retrogressive decision, the House of Lords did not deviate from English orthodoxy in *Walford and Others v Miles and Another.*[34] The husband and wife defendants were the owners of a company and property from where a photographic processing business was carried on. In January 1987 negotiations began between the first and second plaintiffs and the first defendant for the sale of the company and the property. On 17th March 1987 the first defendant orally agreed to deal exclusively with the first plaintiff and to terminate any negotiations then being carried on between the defendants and any other potential purchasers. The only condition was that the plaintiffs provide a "comfort letter" confirming that they had the necessary financial support from their bank to complete any purchase. The condition was complied with. Notwithstanding the "agreement", the defendant subsequently chose to deal with a third party and

---

30 Unrep., 24th February 1992
31 (1984) 465 US 17
32 Civil No. 89-1033-FR, 1989 U.S.DIST.LEXIS 14756
33 Unpub. dissertation by Stephen Pratt, James R. Knowles, Cambridge
34 [1992] 2 A.C 128

completed a sale which excluded the plaintiffs. The plaintiffs sued for breach of contract. The House of Lords held that the agreement of 17th March contained no term as to the duration of the obligation to negotiate with the plaintiffs and made no provision for the defendants to determine the negotiations. Any duty to negotiate in good faith was unworkable and inherently inconsistent with the position of a negotiating party since parties to negotiations were always at liberty to terminate such negotiations at any time and for any reason. The agreement as between the plaintiffs and the defendants was void for uncertainty. It was simply their agreement to negotiate. In the words of Lord Ackner:[35]

> "An agreement to negotiate has no legal content" and "... good faith is inherently repugnant to the adversarial position of the parties when involved in negotiations."

In some respects, there was a superficial similarly between *Walford* and a later Court of Appeal decision, *Pitt v P.H.H. Asset Management Ltd.*[36] The case related to the sale and purchase of a dwelling house. The parties had agreed a "lock-out" arrangement by which the plaintiff should have the opportunity to exchange contracts within two weeks of receipt of the draft, during which the defendant would refrain from negotiating with third parties. The Court of Appeal upheld the "lock-out" arrangement in *Pitt* because it was for a finite period and therefore not uncertain, also sidestepping the question of consideration.

Peter Gibson LJ quoted from Lord Ackner's judgment in *Walford*:[37]

> "There is clearly no reason in the English contract law why A, for good consideration, should not achieve an enforceable agreement whereby B agrees for a specified period of time, not to negotiate with anyone except A in relation to the sale of his property."

and then continued:

> "... B by agreeing not to negotiate for this fixed period with a party, locks himself out of such negotiation. He has in no legal sense locked himself into negotiations with A. What A has achieved is an exclusive opportunity, for a fixed period, to try and come to terms with B, an opportunity for which he has, unless he makes his agreement under seal, to give good consideration."[38]

---

35 at 181–2
36 [1994] 1 WLR 327
37 at 139
38 at 181–2

The Court does have an inherent power to stay any action which it considers should not be allowed to continue and statutory powers under the Supreme Court Act 1981. In addition, certain commentators have identified dicta of Dunn LJ in *Northern Regional Health Authority* v *Derek Crouch Construction Company Ltd*[39] (overruled on other grounds in a 1998 House of Lords decision) as being supportive of the proposition that the courts will uphold a mandatory adjudication provision - and perhaps a suitable mediation clause, in a contract. In the words of Dunn LJ:[40]

> "Where parties have agreed on machinery...for the resolution of disputes, it is not for the court to intervene and replace its own process for the contractual machinery agreed by the parties."

A similar position was adopted by Kerr LJ in *Tubeworkers Ltd* v *Tilbury Construction Ltd.*[41]

The Arbitration Act 1996 contains an important provision which may assist the enforceability of mediation clauses if the contract contains an arbitration clause. Section 9 (1) of the Act gives the Court power to stay court proceedings issued by a party to an arbitration agreement, where the matter in question should fall within the arbitration agreement while section 9(4) calls for a mandatory stay to arbitration if required by the defendant in most cirumstances. However, Section 9 (2) extends this power to stay "notwithstanding that the matter is to be referred to arbitration only after the exhaustion of the dispute resolution procedures". A "tiered" ADR clause (*e.g* mediation, followed by arbitration if the mediation does not result in settlement) may enable a party to that agreement to stay legal proceedings pending completion of the mediation, as well as of the arbitration.

39 [1984] 1 QB 644
40 (1985) 30 BLR 67, at 77, 78
41 (1985) 30 BLR 67, at 77, 78

Putting Alternative Dispute Resolution at the Forefront of Professional Practice

Many litigators still believe that ADR has little or nothing to offer either the legal profession or clients. Similarly, many clients pursuing a claim believe that to propose ADR shows them to be a 'soft touch' lacking confidence in their own case. The number of cases referred to ADR remains depressingly small. Oxford Brooks University surveyed 500 main and sub-contractors in the construction industry to establish their experience of ADR.[1] Approximately 96% had never referred a dispute to ADR although there was no particular hostility towards the process. Many contractors felt that their lawyers were not particularly assertive in suggesting the possible use of ADR. Many litigation lawyers appear to remain complacent about the value of litigation and fail to appreciate the deleterious effect that it may have on their clients' businesses – both in terms of cost and the expenditure of non-productive man hours. According to a letter published in *The Times* newspaper:

> "Our adversarial culture encourages settlement. Ninety-five percent of cases never get to trial. Litigation lawyers recognise that it is their primary function to resolve disputes, and I know of no evidence to support the proposition that the litigation process is deliberately protracted to generate fees."[2]

The writer's second proposition may be generally true, although instances of fee earners deliberately padding client bills to meet their chargeable hours' target without undue injury to their personal lives is not unknown. However, the correctness of the writer's first proposition is questionable. It is equally arguable that the litigation process diverts the parties' attention away from the desirability of settlement until a particular case has progressed to such a stage that a natural process of implosion takes over and the parties are simply

---

1 op.cit.
2 *The Times*, 24 June 1997

relieved to be released from the litigation – often on terms that are not particularly advantageous to them.

Much of the present failure of ADR stems from a belief on the part of many litigators that there is no middle course between negotiation and litigation. These litigators believe they are good negotiators and if they are unsuccessful in negotiating a particular case that means the case is only suitable for resolution by litigation. Lawyers may fail as negotiators because of a desire to stand shoulder to shoulder with their clients and to play the role of hired gun rather than that of objective advisor. Frequently lawyers simply replicate their client's own dysfunctional stance. CEDR has identified some of the reasons for the failure of negotiations as follows:

- poor negotiating skills;
- unrealistic expectations;
- unrealistic assessment of interests or alternatives;
- emotional antagonism or personality clashes (not least between the lawyers);
- desire for revenge;
- distrust;
- failure to communicate;
- inability to decide whether a particular offer is suitable or represents the maximum achievable;
- inability of parties to problem solve;
- gamesmanship and brinksmanship;
- advisors lacking appropriate authority;
- the existence of litigation diverting attention from the negotiations;
- disagreements that quite simply cannot be overcome.

Lawyers are frequently hampered from being good negotiators by failing to take a rounded view of their clients' cases. The lawyer's role is not simply a case of taking the client's instructions (allowing the client to tell his own story in his own words and relying on a selection of documents made by the client). It is also relevant to be able to probe behind the client's ostensible position and identify the hidden agenda or reality which is being avoided. Frequently money claims are not paid simply because the defending party cannot do so, and spurious counterclaims are put forward based on such subjective criteria as goods not being of satisfactory quality. Many lawyers have neither the time nor the experience to evaluate all the particular features which motivate the client telling his story. Again, lawyers are frequently poor negotiators because they commence a negotiation having not made an objective analysis of the client's position, having little or no appreciation of what they wish to achieve via the negotiation and with little or no experience of how to move from the articulation of positions to the achievement of solutions.

A fee earner going to his filing cabinet may wonder how cases can be selected as being suitable for ADR. A checklist to assist with case selection for ADR is included at Appendix 12. Superficially, a fee earner may discount those cases which include points of law as being unsuitable for the mediation process. However, mediation can encompass points of law. If they arise, the mediator will deal with them in a different way from that which a judge or arbitrator would adopt. Although a mediator is principally facilitative, he may on occasions be evaluative. A legally trained mediator may well require a summary of each party's position on a particular point of law, and subsequently test the legitimacy of any views put forward in the caucus sessions. Other issues to be considered in making a case selection for ADR include:

- Does the client honestly wish to bring matters to a head quickly and cheaply? A lawyer acting for a potential defendant may be happy to adopt the litigation route knowing that any counter claim to be put forward is a "paper" one only and simply advanced to delay resolution of the dispute and possibly to wear down a plaintiff. Conversely, a potential plaintiff may have a good arguable case which is ill-suited to summary judgment and where the best solution might extend beyond a simple award of money.

- Litigation may already have been commenced, pleadings exchanged and even discovery and inspection of documents completed. The initial euphoria arising from the exchange of pleadings has gone and both parties might be prepared to look at settlement if they only knew how to do so and overcome the polarisation caused by the litigation.

- Special care needs to be taken if the client is either a public body or backed by insurance. In the case of the latter, a decision to use ADR must have the support of the insurance company. In the case of the former, public bodies crave the scientific approach to their disputes. Either they live in fear or claim to live in fear of their auditors. Initially they state that it is better to go through litigation, however ruinous, than to engage in a settlement process which lacks science and ultimately leads to a piece of horse trading. Overcoming these difficulties is an educative process. Public bodies need to be reminded that most litigation settles following a piece of belated horse trading usually only when high costs have already been incurred.

- Sometimes the full blaze of publicity is best avoided by clients. This is certainly true in many computer software disputes where there is commercial sensitivity perhaps between rival companies or in the case of public authorities where it is better for potentially dirty linen not to be washed in public which might lead to a falling away in public confidence.

- A lawyer may make the assessment that the issues are evenly balanced as between plaintiff and defendant and some sort of compromise will emerge at trial. In such a situation the traditional response has been to make a payment into court to provide some protection in costs. Early resolution of the dispute by ADR offers an alternative approach.

- Cases of wider public significance which will do more than merely establish the private rights and obligations as between two parties will not be suitable for ADR. In this category are those cases which lead to judicial review applications in the High Court. For instance, it may be suitable to deal with the exclusion of a particular unruly child from school in an ADR session although ADR would be quite unsuitable if a child, living in a particular location, had been refused access to a particular school or the provision of school transport. The interests of that child would presumably be co-extensive with those of a class of other children.

- The existence of technical issues does not preclude the use of mediation. A mediation can proceed on the basis that the parties are represented not only by their lawyers but also by a technical expert who can assist the mediator with the technical features of the case. If the mediator is technically unqualified it may be sensible for a legally qualified mediator to sit with a co-mediator from a technical discipline.

- Traditionally ADR appeared unattractive if the claimant or defendant qualified for Legal Aid and a ticket to litigate was seemingly provided by the state. In a landmark decision[3] the Legal Aid Board (LAB) extended non family legal aid cetificates to

3 *Gazette*, 28th October 1998, 95/41

include mediation. According to LAB's costs and appeals committee[4]:

> "We are pleased to have clarified this. The legal aid scheme should allow clients and their lawyers to resolve disputes in the most appropriate and cost-effective way."

Commenting, Law Society President, Michael Matthews, stated[5]:

> "It was always perverse that legal aid was not available for mediation despite the fact the public policy encourages litigants to mediate or use other forms of alternative dispute resolution."

In some cases a mediated solution is self-evidently desirable. For instance, disputes between neighbours, whether over noise or boundaries, require prompt solutions if harmony is to be restored. In addition, such disputes, if litigated, lead to high legal costs and a solution, which is no solution, having been imposed by a judge and lacking the authority to change the fundamental attitudes and behaviour of the participants in the dispute. Judge-made resolution of neighbourhood disputes frequently leads to further acrimony between the parties, fresh applications to court, a further deterioration in relationships and a realisation that one of the parties will end up moving house.

The political reaction to ADR has been equivocal. Some support was given by the last Conservative Government, and prior to taking power the Labour Party published its own discussion document.[6] The essence of the Labour Party document was an assertion that there would be no further funding of litigation via the Legal Aid Fund and other "self-help" mechanisms, such as ADR, would be necessary. In the words of the discussion paper:[7]

> "The present system of publicly funded legal services is costly, inefficient and available to only a small section of society. The system is biased towards traditional, expensive court based legal action rather than other ways of resolving disputes...
>
> It is widely acknowledged that many disputes that are currently resolved through the courts could and should be resolved more satisfactorily, appropriately and cheaply through some means of alternative dispute resolution (ADR). There are some cases where they inevitably require a court hearing to ensure that justice is done, but courts

---

4 *The Guardian*, 28th October 1998
5 *Gazette*, 28th October 1998, 95/41
6 *Access to Justice*, Labour Party Conference, July 1995
7 *ibid*

are not the only place where disputes can be settled. Conflicts at a relatively personal level in particular often benefit from a procedure that is less formal and adversarial, and for plaintiffs for small claims a process such as mediation is a far less hazardous option than litigation. "

In the discussion paper the Labour Party expressed itself far from convinced that legal expenses insurance would provide a suitable way forward, perhaps because it gave a fillip to lawyers fees rather than act to promote the amicable and prompt resolution of disputes. Therefore, it seems approaching the millenium that fee earners will need to look more carefully at the value of ADR to their particular case loads – particularly with the growth in Practice Directions and the possibility that the judiciary will be less sparing in the use of wasted costs' orders against practitioners who needlessly or perhaps incompetently prolong cases following implementation of the Woolf reforms after April 1999.

One of the biggest areas of disputes has been in healthcare.[8] According to Easterbrook:

- Cost of NHS to date estimated £150,000,000
- Average plaintiff's costs of case £22,500
- Average cost of case going to trial £88,000
- £16.5 million recovery for plaintiffs cost £4.5 million
- 12% of medical negligence cases are successful
- In 1995 there were 12,000 medical negligence cases
- The cost to the Legal Aid Board for medical negligence cases in 1995 was £24,000,000
- To 1996 there had been a 15% rise per annum in claims against doctors from medical negligence
- 95% of medical negligence claims are legally aided

A particular example of mediation in healthcare was cited by the author. First, the article referred to a Department of Health two-year mediation pilot scheme in Oxford, Anglia, Northern and Yorkshire regions. The given examples of mediation were as follows. First, a woman who lost a child as a result of an infection was settled in a day with costs in the region of £10,000 and an undisclosed payment of compensation in the woman's favour. In a second case, again concerning obstetrics, the patient felt that she had been badly treated but the experience of meeting face to face with the obstetrician during the course of mediation apparently assisted the

---

8 *Solicitors Journal*, 26th April 1996, J. Easterbrook, pp. 410–11

transformation of the relationship between plaintiff and defendant back into a clinical one rather than simply to remain one being based on antagonism.

Once a fee earner has decided that his case is suitable for ADR he is left with the problem what to do next. ADR is still not part of either our legal or commercial "culture". Fee earners remain reluctant to propose ADR: then, it is a voyage into the unknown. For party A to suggest ADR to party B, who refuses to pay up, may be seen as a sign of weakness. The plaintiff can be derided – if he had confidence in his case he would simply get on with the process of litigating. The fee earner may stumble to explain to an unyielding opponent the benefits to both parties of ADR but without achieving any real support for the proposition. To overcome this impasse some people suggest that a third-party intermediary, such as CEDR, may be asked to approach the opponent to explain the virtues of ADR and potentially to bypass the obstructiveness of the opponent's lawyers. On occasions, the fee earner will find himself with an opponent who knows of ADR and is committed to the process as an effective means of resolving disputes. In that situation it is much easier to set up an ADR session. Short of a "culture" change[9] and ADR being genuinely client driven, the simplest method of getting parties to engage in ADR is via a clause in the contract which gave rise to the dispute in the first place. Therefore, it is essential to check the dispute clause in the particular contract to see whether or not the recalcitrant opponent can be knocked into line by stating that the parties have already agreed ADR as the method of resolving their disputes.

The judiciary remains ambivalent about mandating courts to comply parties to consider ADR, although it now seems inevitable that a failure to follow an ADR procedure, where applicable, will become a material circumstance to be considered on the entitlement to and quantum of costs. How effectively such a sanction can be imposed time will tell:[10]

> "Speaking at a Centre for Dispute Resolution Forum, Sir Richard Scott ruled out the prospect of the courts directing mandatory mediation to replace conventional litigation. It was a constitutional issue of great

---

9 In some countries and societies there is a profound social or religious bias in favour of ADR. Confucianism pervades Far Eastern societies and, nearer home, the Beth Din (the rabbinical court) has promoted ADR. Without a social or religious dimension ADR is inevitably harder to sell in The United Kingdom.

10 "No Mandatory ADR", *The Litigation Letter*, May 1998, p.41

importance that any democratic society was obliged to make a judicial system for civil disputes available to both individual and corporate bodies. There should be no sanction on parties wishing to litigate instead of mediating. He was in favour of encouragment only, although he envisaged that any litigation proceedings already under way could be stayed in order to provide a window for ADR to take place. And if mediation was not successful, court proceedings could recommence.

LSG 25 March

Comment: *Sir Richard's remarks are at a variance with the consultative new Costs Rules which provide for the parties' conduct during litigation, including 'unreasonable' refusal to participate in ADR, as being relevant both as to the entitlement and to the quantum of costs. It is also at variance with the comments of the Master of the Rolls, Lord Woolf, at a recent seminar, that although a plaintiff had the right to go to court and not to an ombudsman if he wanted, if the other party was perfectly prepared to cooperate with going to the ombudsman, perhaps this should be a matter which the court should be able to take into account in deciding whether a particular order for costs was appropriate. He suggested ombudsmen could resolve disputes which courts could not decide 'proportionately'."*

Once the decision to mediate a dispute has been taken or mediation is the prescribed route under the contract, organisational arrangements should be easier. If the obligation to mediate is based on a contract term, the contract may prescribe the manner in which the mediation is to be organised. It may, for instance, require disputes or differences to be referred to mediation under the auspices of CEDR in accordance with the CEDR Model Mediation Procedure in force for the time being. If that is the case there are no further discretions to be exercised by the parties unless they decide to deviate by agreement from what was previously agreed. If the contract, although requiring ADR, is silent on the procedures to be adopted or if the parties, without a contractual requirement to mediate, decide to mediate their dispute, then once the principle of ADR has been agreed they will need to decide upon an ADR procedure. If this is the case, they will have to decide on the appointment of the third party neutral or, in the absence of agreement, identify the appointing body which will carry out this task on their behalf. In addition, if standard procedures of the type proposed by CEDR or the Chartered Institute of Arbitrators are rejected, the parties may have the expensive and potentially delaying need to resolve, as a preliminary issue, the procedures to be adopted between them. For the inexperienced user of ADR it is probably preferable to use standard procedures than to be left with a whole checklist of issues needing to be resolved. In the absence of standard procedures, the parties will need to consider the following:

- In the absence of agreement as to the neutral's appointment, which appointing body will carry out the task on their joint behalf?

- Is the mediator required to have special skills (either technical or legal)?

- The venue for the mediation.

- Whether the dispute will be referred to mediation or some other of the ADR techniques (executive tribunal, conciliation, etc.).

- Is the mediation subject to time limits? If resolution is not achieved within a prescribed period does the mediation automatically come to an end? Is it to be part of the agreement to mediate that during the currency of the mediation phase the right to instigate proceedings in litigation or arbitration is suspended?

- All the operational details for the mediation. Are position papers to be submitted to the mediatior in advance by the parties? If so, are those position papers to be of a prescribed length? Once the mediation commences, are the parties to be given in open session a limited period of time to expand upon the points made in the position papers? Are the costs of the mediation to be split on a 50:50 basis as regards the mediator's appointment – with each party responsible for its own technical and other costs?

- Is the mediator simply to be a facilitator – where if the parties fail to come to their own agreement the mediation is aborted? Alternatively, if the mediation is unsuccessful is the mediator to be empowered to make a recommendation of the type anticipated by the ICE Conciliation Procedure (1994)? This has the advantage of putting some punch into the mediation process. Parties who cannot resolve their differences often find, when left with a conciliator's recommendation, and having thought about matters coolly, the recommendation is not so bad after all and the uncertainties of litigation or arbitration cannot be justified.

- How are potentially complicated collateral legal issues to be resolved? Rather than rely upon the potential vagaries of the general law, should the parties decide in advance that the mediator is to be non-compellable in any subsequent litigation or arbitration? If the third-party neutral is required to provide (in the absence of agreement) a recommendation, what is the status of that recommendation in subsequent litigation or arbitration? Is it to be a disclosable document to the judge or arbitrator or to be considered as part of a without prejudice process? It may also be sensible for the parties to decide in advance of the mediation what happens to any personal notes (including those of the third-party neutral) made during the course of the mediation. The best way to avoid future disputes (if there is litigation) about the discoverability of such documents is to agree in advance that at the end of the mediation, whether successful or not, all such notes will be destroyed before the parties leave.

- It may be sensible to agree by whom the parties are to be represented in order to avoid pointless conflict when the mediation commences. Always agree in advance if lawyers or technical experts are to be present. Again, it is important to ensure there is equality of representation as regards the status of management present. Even if the prime players will be those responsible for the dispute in the first place and for its subsequent management, it is useful that at the hearing the parties are also represented by a higher level of management, detached from the dispute, able to take hard decisions that settlement may entail and able to climb down from untenable positions.

- The role of the lawyers must be clearly established. Are lawyers to draft the opening statements and make the initial oral representations to the mediator before the mediator goes into private caucus sessions with each of the parties? Alternatively, are the parties to run the mediation themselves, reducing the involvement of lawyers to a "support" service, simply there to assist the mediator with any points of law that arise during the course of the mediation and ready to draft, as necessary, terms of settlement?

- Lawyers need to decide how much preparation is required for a mediation. Mediation is not a substitute for proper case preparation although the method of preparation may be different from that required in litigation or arbitration. Without allowing the documentation to get out of hand, the lawyers require access to a sufficiently large number of documents to make an intelligent assessment of the case and this may involve agreeing with the other side a process by which, prior to the mediation, a limited form of discovery and inspection of documents occurs. Preparing for a mediation will involve taking proper witness statements early rather than late with lawyers perhaps in a more assertive role than they play in litigation – genuinely testing the propositions put forward to them by clients. Although clients may be accustomed to withholding information from their own lawyers, mediation cannot succeed on that basis. During the caucus sessions, a skilled mediator will wish to explore a party's ostensible position and coax that party to relinquish those elements of the stated position which are not tenable. It is best for a party's lawyer to have a clear idea prior to the mediation that certain arguments are weak and will not survive detailed testing during the caucus sessions.

The future value of ADR as a means for the resolution of commercial disputes in the United Kingdom remains a matter of some conjecture. After some six or seven years of sustained effort, the number of disputes which are resolved (in the absence of informal negotiations) by ADR remains – for the proponents of ADR – somewhat depressing. Perhaps part of the problem rests with legal practitioners. They have spent countless years encouraging parties to litigate so why should such parties now instantly follow the clarion call of those suggesting that there is a more sensible method? Second, the impact of economic recession at particular times in the 1990s has not necessarily meant clients reaching for their lawyers with an increase in the number of writs and county court summonses issued although the traditional perception is that clients throw money at collecting debts in difficult periods. At such times, clients are just as likely to do deals personally rather than reach for the unknown and not cost free ADR. Third, it has been suggested that, just as the United Kingdom is becoming more interested in ADR, interest in the United states of America is lessening. However, this does not appear to be a proposition that can be seriously advanced. It is, of course, imprudent though to draw too many comparisons between the United Kingdom and the United States. Legal practice in the American civil courts is very different from that in England and Wales. The development of ADR in the United States has been encouraged by the particular costs' regime found in the American courts, the lack of adequate peremptory remedies of the RSC Order 14 variety and the use of juries for the resolution of what may be complex commercial disputes. Clearly these features are not present in England and Wales. Again, time will tell whether *Access to*

Justice,[11] tighter management systems in the courts, the requirements of the *Practice Note (Civil Litigation: Case Management)*[12] and other developments, including construction industry adjudication under the Housing Grants Construction and Regeneration Act 1996, the CPR operational from 26 April 1999 and conditional fees, will render ADR a revolution that never quite had its day but an insurrection leading to necessary changes in the *ancien régime*. That said, litigation and arbitration will always draw to them a substantial element of formality (with costs and time consequences) which ADR-based solutions should be able to avoid, leaving the latter perhaps better equipped to meet the needs of intelligent businessmen as we approach the millennium.

In conclusion, ADR represents a new and exciting challenge for lawyers: its time will probably come with mandatory ADR (whether overt or through the back door) and although not currently part of the political agenda the mandatory imposition of ADR in the future cannot be disregarded. ADR will be a voyage of discovery for many legal practitioners and attract the same scepticism as attended the efforts of early explorers and travellers. The comments of the Roman historian Tacitus[13] are instructive and portray the attitude of suspicion with which ADR is viewed in many quarters:

> "*Nunc terminus Britanniae patet, atque omne ignotum pro magnifico est.*"

or in more popular terms:

> "If in doubt don't touch it."

---

11 Final Report to the Lord Chancellor on the Civil Justice System in England and Wales, Lord Woolf, July 1996, Interim Report to the Lord Chancellor on the Civil Justice System in England and Wales, Lord Woolf, June 1995, Section I, para. 18 and Section II, papra 16(c) of the Final Report.
12 [1995] 1 All ER 385
13 Agricola, Chap. 30

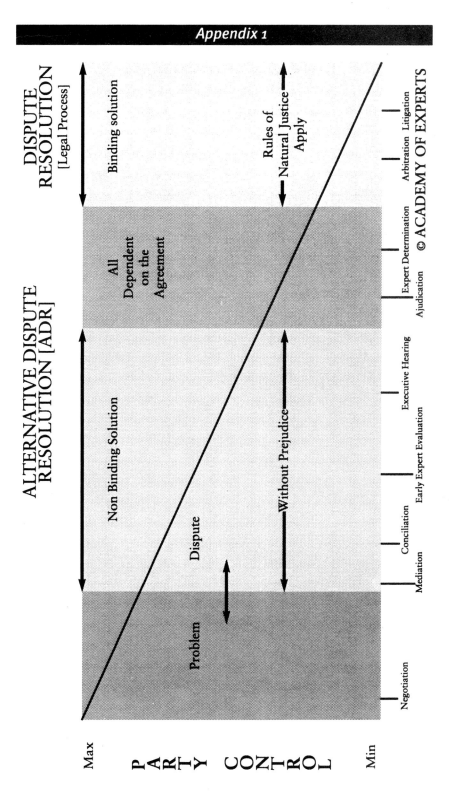

Practice Direction (Civil Litigation: Case Management)

1. The paramount importance of reducing the cost and delay of civil litigation makes it necessary for judges sitting at first instance to assert greater control over the preparation for and conduct of hearings than has hitherto been customary. Failure by practitioners to conduct cases economically will be visited by appropriate orders for costs, including wasted costs orders.

2. The court will accordingly exercise its discretion to limit (a) discovery; (b) the length of oral submissions; (c) the time allowed for the examination and cross-examination of witnesses; (d) the issues on which it wishes to be addressed; (e) reading aloud from documents and authorities.

3. Unless otherwise ordered, every witness statement shall stand as the evidence in chief of the witness concerned.

4. RSC, Ord. 18, r. 7 (facts, not evidence, to be pleaded) will be strictly enforced. In advance of trial parties should use their best endeavours to agree which are the issues or the main issues, and it is their duty so far as possible to reduce or eliminate the expert issues.

5. RSC, Ord. 34, r. 10(2)(a) to (c) (the court bundle) will also be strictly enforced. Documents for use in court should be in A4 format where possible, contained in suitably secured bundles, and lodged with the court at least two clear days before the hearing of an application or a trial. Each bundle should be paginated, indexed, wholly legible, and arranged chronologically and contained in a ring binder or a lever-arch file. Where documents are copied unnecessarily or bundled incompetently the cost will be disallowed.

6. In cases estimated to last for more than 10 days a pre-trial review should be applied for or in default may be appointed by the court. It should when practicable be conducted by the trial judge between eight and four weeks before the date of trial and should be attended by the advocates who are to represent the parties at trial.

7. Unless the court otherwise orders, there must be lodged with the listing officer (or equivalent) on behalf of each party no later than two months before the date of trial a completed pre-trial check-list in the form annexed to this practice direction.

8. Not less than three clear days before the hearing of an action or application each party should lodge with the court (with copies to other parties) a skeleton argument concisely summarising that party's submissions in relation to each of the issues, and citing the main authorities relied upon

which may be attached. Skeleton arguments should be as brief as the nature of the issues allows, and should not without leave of the court exceed 20 pages of double-spaced A4 paper.

9. The opening speech should be succinct. At its conclusion other parties may be invited briefly to amplify their skeleton arguments. In a heavy case the court may in conjunction with final speeches require written submissions, including the findings of fact for which each party contends.

10. This direction applies to all lists in the Queen's Bench and Chancery Divisions, except where other directions specifically apply.

LORD TAYLOR OF GOSFORTH CJ
SIR RICHARD SCOTT V-C

24 January 1995

PRE-TRIAL CHECK-LIST

[Short title of action, folio number]
[Trial date]
[Party lodging check-list]
[Name of solicitor]
[Name(s) of counsel for trial (if known)]

Setting down
1. Has the action been set down?

Pleadings
2. (a) Do you intend to make any amendment to your pleading? (b) If so, when?

Interrogatories
3. (a) Are any interrogatories outstanding? (b) If so, when served and upon whom?

Evidence
4. (a) Have all orders in relation to expert, factual and hearsay evidence been complied with? If not, specify what remains outstanding. (b) Do you intend to serve/seek leave to serve/any further report or statement? If so, when and what report or statement? (c) Have all other orders in relation to oral evidence been complied with? (d) Do you require any further leave or orders in relation to evidence? If so, please specify and say when will you apply.

5. (a) What witnesses of fact do you intend to call? [Names] (b) What expert witnesses do you intend to call? [Names] (c) Will any witness require an interpreter? If so, which?

Documents

6. (a) Have all orders in relation to discovery been complied with? (b) If not, what orders are outstanding? (c) Do you intend to apply for any further orders relating to discovery? (d) If so, what and when?
7. Will you not later than seven days before trial have prepared agreed paginated bundles of fully legible documents for the use of counsel and the court?

Pre-trial review

8. (a) Has a pre-trial review been ordered? (b) If so, when is it to take place? (c) If not, would it be useful to have one?

Length of trial

9. What are counsels' estimates of the minimum and maximum lengths of the trial? [The answer to question 9 should ordinarily be supported by an estimate of length signed by the counsel to be instructed.]

Alternative dispute resolution

   (see *Practice Statement (Commercial Cases: Alternative Dispute Resolution)* [1994] I WLR 14).

10. Have you or counsel discussed with your client(s) the possibility of attempting to resolve this dispute (or particular issues) by alternative dispute resolution ("ADR")?
11. Might some form of ADR procedure assist to resolve or narrow the issues in this case?
12. Have you or your client(s) explored with the other parties the possibility of resolving this dispute (or particular issues) by ADR?

[Signature of the solicitor, date]

Note: This check-list must be lodged not later than two months before the date of hearing with copies to the other parties.

Suggested ADR Paragraphs

Modified "Calderbank"

(1) This is formally to advise you that we are offering to mediate in this case.

We make this proposal on the basis that we reserve the right to draw the Court's attention to it on the subject of costs if the dispute proceeds via litigation.

(2) We propose that this matter is one suitable for resolution via a mediation process. We therefore invite you to agree in principle that the matter be resolved via ADR.

We make this proposal on the basis that we reserve the right to draw the Court's attention to it on the subject of costs if the dispute proceeds via litigation.

© ADR Group

Practice Statement (Commercial Cases: Alternative Dispute Resolution) (No. 2)

On 10 December 1993 Cresswell J. issued *Practice Statement (Commercial Cases: Alternative Dispute Resolution)* [1994] 1 WLR 14 on the subject of alternative dispute resolution ("ADR") indicating that the judges of the Commercial Court wished to encourage parties to consider the use of ADR. In consequence of that practice statement, amendments were made to the standard questions to be answered by the parties in preparation for the summons for directions and to the standard questions to be answered as part of the pre-trial check list. Additional questions were inserted in order to direct the attention of the parties and their legal advisers to ADR as a means of settling their disputes (see *Practice Direction (Commercial Court: Practice Guide)* [1994] 1 WLR 1270). By that practice direction, legal advisers were urged to ensure that parties were fully informed as to the most cost effective means of resolving the particular dispute.

The judges of the Commercial Court in conjunction with the Commercial Court Committee have recently considered whether it is now desirable that any further steps should be taken to encourage the wider use of ADR as a means of settling disputes pending before the court. In the belief that, whereas the Commercial Court will remain an entirely appropriate forum for resolving most of the disputes which are commenced before it, the settlement of actions by means of ADR (i) significantly helps to save litigants the ever-mounting cost of bringing their cases to trial, (ii) saves them the delay of litigation in reaching finality in their disputes; (iii) enables them to achieve settlement of their disputes while preserving their existing commercial relationship and market reputation: (iv) provides them with a wider range of settlement solutions than those offered by litigation; and (v) is likely to make a substantial contribution to the more efficient use of judicial resources, the judges will henceforth adopt the following practice on the hearing of the first *inter partes* summons at which directions for the interlocutory progress of the action arc given or at subsequent *inter partes* hearings at which such directions are sought.

If it should appear to the judge that the action before him or any of the issues arising in it are particularly appropriate for an attempt at settlement by ADR techniques but that the parties have not previously attempted settlement by such means, he may invite the parties to take positive steps to set in motion ADR procedures. The judge may, if he considers it appropriate, adjourn the proceedings then before him for a specified period of time to encourage and enable the parties to take such steps. He may for this purpose extend the time for compliance by the parties or either of them with any requirement under the Rules of the Supreme Court or previous interlocutory orders in the proceedings.

If, after discussion with those representing the parties, it appears to the judge that an early neutral evaluation is likely to assist in the resolution of the matters in dispute, he may offer to provide that evaluation himself or to arrange for another judge to do so. If that course is accepted by the parties, the judge may thereupon give directions as to such preparatory steps for that evaluation and the form which it is to take as he considers appropriate. The parties will in that event be required to arrange with the Commercial Court Listing Office the time for the evaluation hearing having regard to the availability of the judge concerned.

Where early neutral evaluation is provided by a judge, that judge will, unless the parties otherwise agree, take no further part in the proceedings either for the purpose of the hearing of summonses or as trial judge.

Except where an early neutral evaluation is to be provided by a judge, the parties will be responsible for agreeing upon a neutral for the purposes of ADR and will be responsible for his fees and expenses. As indicated in *Practice Statement (Commercial Cases: Alternative Dispute Resolution)* [1994] 1 WLR 14 made by Cresswell J. on 10 December 1993, the Clerk to the Commercial Court keeps a list of individuals and bodies that offer mediation, conciliation and other ADR services. If, after ADR has been recommended to them by the judge, the parties are unable to agree upon a neutral for ADR they may by consent refer to the judge for assistance in reaching such agreement.

On the hearing of any summons in the course of which the judge invites the parties to take steps to resolve their differences by ADR he may on that occasion make such order as to the costs that the parties may incur by reason of their using or attempting to use ADR as may in all the circumstances seem appropriate.

Should the parties be unable to resolve their differences by ADR or otherwise within the period of any such adjournment as may be ordered, they may restore the summons for directions or other summons for the purpose of reporting back to the judge what progress has been made by way of ADR (such report to cover only the process adopted and its outcome, not the substantive contact between the parties and their advisers) and whether further time is required for the purposes of ADR and, where efforts towards settlement by means of ADR have proved fruitless, for the purpose of obtaining further interlocutory directions in the proceedings.

Parties to pending proceedings who consider that ADR might be an appropriate form of dispute resolution for those proceedings or who wish to discuss the applicability of ADR with a commercial judge will be strongly encouraged to bring on the summons for directions at an earlier stage in the proceedings than would otherwise be justifiable. The fact that in such a case pleadings have not yet closed or that discovery has not yet been completed will not be regarded by the court as a reason for declining to consider the applicability of ADR in that case.

WALLER J
Judge in charge of the Commercial List

7 June 1996

Practice Direction: Medical Negligence

1. From 1 November 1996, Master Foster has been assigned to hear all interlocutory applications in actions involving claims arising out of allegations of medical/clinical negligence.

2. The following arrangements will apply to all such actions to which a Master has not been assigned prior to 1 November 1996.

3. (a) The Plaintiff in such actions must issue a summons for directions within 28 days of the close of pleadings and shall mark the summons in the bottom right hand corner "medical negligence". On seeking a hearing for the summons, the counter staff in Room E2 14 are to be told that the case involves allegations of medical negligence.
   (b) The Plaintiff shall serve with a copy of the summons
       (i) a summary description of the action limited to 250 words and
       (ii) a chronology of material events in the form of a schedule.
   (c) The Defendant shall within 14 days of receipt of a copy of the summons
       (i) produce an initial list of outstanding issues limited to 250 words
       (ii) comment on the Plaintiff's chronology.

4. Such applications will be listed before Master Foster on Tuesdays or Fridays within 28 days of issue. In the Vacation, the summons will be listed within 28 days of the start of the next term or will be taken by one of the Vacation Masters.

5. At the first hearing of the summons for directions:
   (a) Each party shall produce an initial list of their potential witnesses as to fact.
   (b) Each party shall specify the number and discipline of the experts it currently intends to rely on, when their reports will be available and the issues to which they will be directed.
   (c) Each party must state whether Alternative Dispute Resolution has been considered and if not why not and if Alternative Dispute Resolution has been rejected why this is so.
   (d) Paragraphs 1-12 and 19 of Practice Form 50 will be dealt with and a date fixed for dealing with the remaining directions including updating the list of issues and the listing of admissions. This date will be shortly after the latest date for exchange of expert's reports and witness statements.

6. The documents referred to in paragraph 3(b) and 3(c) above should be lodged with Master Foster at least 48 hours before the time fixed for hearing the summons for directions.

7. All time summonses in medical negligence cases after 1 November 1996 will be heard:
   (a) In term, by Master Foster at 10 am on Tuesdays and Fridays
   (b) In Vacation, in accordance with the current practice

8. In all medical negligence actions the Plaintiff should serve each intended Defendant with a letter before action, at least 3 months before issue of the Writ. Such letter should set out the fullest available information as to the basis of the claim. If the Plaintiff does not serve such a letter then the Court may grant an appropriate extension of time to the Defendant for serving a Defence.

9. The hearing of all summonses (other than time summonses) in medical negligence actions must be attended by the solicitor in charge of the case or counsel instructed therein. If, for good reason, this is not possible a fully briefed deputy may attend. However, if the summons cannot be dealt with properly because of the deputy's lack of familiarity with the case, a wasted costs order may be made.

Signed: R L Turner
Senior Master, Queen's Bench Division

16 October 1996

WIPO Mediation Rules

(Effective from October 1, 1994)

CONTENTS

ABBREVIATED EXPRESSIONS

Article 1

In these Rules:

"Mediation Agreement" means an agreement by the parties to submit to mediation all or certain disputes which have arisen or which may arise between them; a Mediation Agreement may be in the form of a mediation clause in a contract or in the form of a separate contract;

"Mediator" includes a sole mediator or all the mediators where more than one is appointed;

"WIPO" means the World Intellectual Property Organization;

"Center" means the WIPO Arbitration Center, a unit of the International Bureau of WIPO.

Words used in the singular include the plural and vice versa, as the context may require.

SCOPE OF APPLICATION OF RULES

Article 2

Where a Mediation Agreement provides for mediation under the WIPO Mediation Rules, these Rules shall be deemed to form part of that Mediation Agreement. Unless the parties have agreed otherwise, these

Rules as in effect on the date of the commencement of the mediation shall apply.

COMMENCEMENT OF THE MEDIATION

Article 3

(a) A party to a Mediation Agreement that wishes to commence a mediation shall submit a Request for Mediation in writing to the Center. It shall at the same time send a copy of the Request for Mediation to the other party.

(b) The Request for Mediation shall contain or be accompanied by
  (i) the names, addresses and telephone, telex, telefax or other communication references of the parties to the dispute and of the representative of the party filing the Request for Mediation;
  (ii) a copy of the Mediation Agreement; and
  (iii) a brief statement of the nature of the dispute.

Article 4

The date of the commencement of the mediation shall be the date on which the Request for Mediation is received by the Center.

Article 5

The Center shall forthwith inform the parties in writing of the receipt by it of the Request for Mediation and of the date of the commencement of the mediation.

APPOINTMENT OF THE MEDIATOR

Article 6

(a) Unless the parties have agreed themselves on the person of the mediator or on another procedure for appointing the mediator, the mediator shall be appointed by the Center after consultation with the parties.

(b) The prospective mediator shall, by accepting appointment, be deemed to have undertaken to make available sufficient time to enable the mediation to be conducted expeditiously.

Article 7

The mediator shall be neutral, impartial and independent.

PRESENTATION OF PARTIES AND PARTICIPATION IN MEETINGS

Article 8

(a) The parties may be represented or assisted in their meetings with the mediator.

(b) Immediately after the appointment of the mediator, the names and addresses of persons authorized to represent a party, and the names and positions of the persons who will be attending the meetings of the parties with the mediator on behalf of that party, shall be communicated by that party to the other party, the mediator and the Center.

CONDUCT OF THE MEDIATION

Article 9

The mediation shall be conducted in the manner agreed by the parties. If, and to the extent that, the parties have not made such agreement, the mediator shall, in accordance with these Rules, determine the manner in which the mediation shall be conducted.

Article 10

Each party shall cooperate in good faith with the mediator to advance the mediation as expeditiously as possible.

Article 11

The mediator shall be free to meet and to communicate separately with a party on the clear understanding that information given at such meetings and in such communications shall not be disclosed to the other party without the express authorization of the party giving the information.

Article 12

(a) As soon as possible after being appointed, the mediator shall, in consultation with the parties, establish a timetable for the submission by each party to the mediator and to the other party of a statement summarising the background of the dispute, the party's interests and contentions in relation to the dispute and the present status of the dispute, together with such other information and materials as the party considers necessary for the purposes of the mediation and, in particular, to enable the issues in dispute to be identified.

(b) The mediator may, at any time during the mediation, suggest that a party provide such additional information or materials as the mediator deems useful.

(c) Any party may at any time submit to the mediator, for consideration by the mediator only, written information or materials which it considers to be confidential. The mediator shall not, without the written authorization of that party, disclose such information or materials to the other party.

ROLE OF THE MEDIATOR

Article 13

(a) The mediator shall promote the settlement of the issues in dispute between the parties in any manner that the mediator believes to be appropriate, but shall have no authority to impose a settlement on the parties.

(b) Where the mediator believes that any issues in dispute between the parties are not susceptible to resolution through mediation, the mediator may propose, for the consideration of the parties, procedures or means for resolving those issues which the mediator considers are most likely, having regard to the circumstances of the dispute and any business relationship between the parties, to lead to the most efficient, least costly and most productive settlement of those issues. In particular, the mediator may so propose:

(i)   an expert determination of one or more particular issues;

(ii) arbitration;

(iii) the submission of last offers of settlement by each party and, in the absence of a settlement through mediation, arbitration conducted on the basis of those last offers pursuant to an arbitral procedure in which the mission of the arbitral tribunal is confined to determining which of the last offers shall prevail; or

(iv) arbitration in which the mediator will, with the express consent of the parties, act as sole arbitrator, it being understood that the mediator may, in the arbitral proceedings, take into account information received during the mediation.

CONFIDENTIALITY

Article 14

No recording of any kind shall be made of any meetings of the parties with the mediator.

Article 15

Each person involved in the mediation, including, in particular, the mediator, the parties and their representatives and advisors, any independent experts and any other persons present during the meetings of the parties with the mediator, shall respect the confidentiality of the mediation and may not, unless otherwise agreed by the parties and the mediator, use or disclose to any outside party any information concerning, or obtained in the course of, the mediation. Each such person shall sign an appropriate confidentiality undertaking prior to taking part in the mediation.

Article 16

Unless otherwise agreed by the parties, each person involved in the mediation shall, on the termination of the mediation, return, to the party providing it, any brief, document or other materials supplied by a party, without retaining any copy thereof. Any notes taken by a person concerning the meetings of the parties with the mediator shall be destroyed on the termination of the mediation.

Article 17

Unless otherwise agreed by the parties, the mediator and the parties shall not introduce as evidence or in any manner whatsoever in any judicial or arbitration proceeding:

(i)   any views expressed or suggestions made by a party with respect to a possible settlement of the dispute;

(ii) any admissions made by a party in the course of the mediation;

(iii) any proposals made or views expressed by the mediator;

(iv) the fact that a party had or had not indicated willingness to accept any proposal for settlement made by the mediator or by the other party.

TERMINATION OF THE MEDIATION

Article 18

The mediation shall be terminated
(i) by the signing of a settlement agreement by the parties covering any or all of the issues in dispute between the parties;
(ii) by the decision of the mediator if, in the mediator's judgement, further efforts at mediation are unlikely to lead to a resolution of the dispute;
(iii) by a written declaration of a party at any time after attending the first meeting of the parties with the mediator and before the signing of any settlement agreement.

Article 19

(a) Upon the termination of the mediation, the mediator shall promptly send to the Center a notice in writing that the mediation is terminated and shall indicate the date on which it terminated, whether or not the mediation resulted in a settlement of the dispute and, if so, whether the settlement was full or partial. The mediator shall send to the parties a copy of the notice so addressed to the Center.
(b) The Center shall keep the said notice of the mediator confidential and shall not, without the written authorization of the parties, disclose either the existence or the result of the mediation to any person.
(c) The Center may, however, include information concerning the mediation in any aggregate statistical data that it publishes concerning its activities

provided that such information does not reveal the identity of the parties or enable the particular circumstances of the dispute to be identified.

Article 20

Unless required by a court of law or authorized in writing by the parties, the mediator shall not act in any capacity whatsoever, otherwise than as a mediator, in any pending or future proceedings, whether Judicial, arbitral or otherwise, relating to the subject matter of the dispute.

REGISTRATION FEE OF THE CENTER

Article 21

(a) The Request for Mediation shall be subject to the payment to the Center of a registration fee, which shall belong to the International Bureau of WIPO. The amount of the registration fee shall be fixed in accordance with the Schedule of Fees applicable on the date of the Request for Mediation.
(b) The registration fee shall not be refundable.
(c) No action shall be taken by the Center on a Request for Mediation until the registration fee has been paid.
(d) If a party who has filed a Request for Mediation fails, within 15 days after a second reminder in writing from the Center, to pay the registration fee, it shall be deemed to have withdrawn its Request for Mediation.

FEES OF THE MEDIATOR

Article 22

(a) The amount and currency of the fees of the mediator and the modalities and timing of their payment shall be fixed, in accordance with the provisions of this Article, by the Center, after consultation with the mediator and the parties.

(b) The amount of the fees shall, unless the parties and the mediator agree otherwise, be calculated on the basis of the hourly or, if applicable, daily indicative rates set out in the Schedule of Fees applicable on the date of the Request for Mediation, taking into account the amount in dispute, the complexity of the subject-matter of the dispute and any other relevant circumstances of the case.

DEPOSITS

Article 23

(a) The Center may, at the time of the appointment of the mediator, require each party to deposit an equal amount as an advance for the costs of the mediation, including, in particular, the estimated fees of the mediator and the other expenses of the mediation. The amount of the deposit shall be determined by the Center.

(b) The Center may require the parties to make supplementary deposits.

(c) If a party fails, within 15 days after a second reminder in writing from the Center, to pay the required deposit, the mediation shall be deemed to be terminated. The Center shall, by notice in writing, inform the parties

and the mediator accordingly and indicate the date of termination.

(d) After the termination of the mediation, the Center shall render an accounting to the parties of any deposits made and return any unexpended balance to the parties or require the payment of any amount owing from the parties.

COSTS

Article 24

Unless the parties agree otherwise, the registration fee, the fees of the mediator and all other expenses of the mediation, including, in particular the required travel expenses of the mediator and any expenses associated with obtaining expert advice, shall be borne in equal shares by the parties.

EXCLUSION OF LIABILITY

Article 25

Except in respect of deliberate wrongdoing, the mediator, WIPO and the Center shall not be liable to any party for any act or omission in connection with any mediation conducted under these Rules.

WAIVER OF DEFAMATION

Article 26

The parties and, by accepting appointment, the mediator agree that any statements or comments, whether written or oral, made or used by them or their representatives in preparation for or in the course of the mediation shall not be relied upon to found or maintain any action for defamation, libel, slander or any related complaint, and this Article may be pleaded in bar to any such action.

SUSPENSION OF RUNNING OF LIMITATION PERIOD UNDER THE STATUTE OF LIMITATIONS

Article 27

The parties agree that, to the extent permitted by the applicable law, the running of the limitation period under the Statute of Limitations or an equivalent law shall be suspended in relation to the dispute that is the subject of the mediation from the date of the commencement of the mediation until the date of the termination of the mediation.

SCHEDULE OF FEES

(All amounts are in United States dollars)

FEES OF THE CENTER

Registration Fee
(Article 21, WIPO Mediation Rules)

1. The amount of the registration fee shall be 0.10% of the value of the mediation, subject to a maximum registration fee of $10,000. By way of example, the following registration fees would be payable where the value of the mediation is the following amounts:

Value of Mediation	Registration Fee
$500,000	$500
$1,000,000	$1,000
$5,000,000	$5,000
$10,000,000 and above	$10,000

2. The value of the mediation is determined by the total value of amounts claimed.

3. Where the Request for Mediation does not indicate any claims for a monetary amount or the dispute concerns issues that are not quantifiable in monetary amounts, a registration fee of $750 shall be payable, subject to adjustment. The adjustment shall be made by reference to the registration fee that the Center, after consultation with the parties and the mediator, determines in its discretion to be appropriate in the circumstances.

4. Any monetary amounts in dispute expressed in currencies other than United States dollars shall, for the purposes of calculating the registration fee, be converted to amounts expressed in United States dollars on the basis of the official United Nations exchange rate prevailing on the date of submission of the Request for Mediation.

MEDIATORS' FEES

Indicative Hourly and Daily Rates
(Article 22, WIPO Mediation Rules)

	Minimum	Maximum
Per hour	$300	$600
Per day	$1,500	$3,500

© WIPO

Centre for Dispute Resolution: Model ADR Contract Clauses (1996)

Including a clause in a contract which requires the parties to attempt to settle any dispute by some form of ADR increases the chances of settling disputes arising out of that contract before, or notwithstanding that, the parties resort to court proceedings or arbitration.

This note consists of:

- A "fast track drafting guide" to the key ADR clauses
- Model contract clauses
- Commentary on each clause as to why it has been suggested, when it should be included and the pros and cons of including it.

Fast track drafting guide

Objective	Use clause
Voluntary mediation – the parties can walk away from the mediation at any time	2
"If any dispute arises out of this agreement the parties will attempt to settle it by mediation in accordance with the Centre for Dispute Resolution's (CEDR) Model Mediation Procedure."	
This wording by itself may be all that is strictly necessary.	
Negotiation before mediation	1
Using CEDR to sort out disagreements about the mediation agreement breaking deadlocks	5
Keeping the option of interim legal remedies	7.4
Obligatory mediation – no litigation/arbitration until after mediation hearing	8
Executive Tribunal	10
Arbitration as a fallback	11

Wording such as "the parties" and "this agreement" may need to be adapted to the definitions in the contract. Square brackets indicate wording on which a view needs to be taken e.g. as to how long a period should be specified or as to whether to include the particular wording at all.

NEGOTIATION

1. If any dispute arises out of this agreement the parties will attempt to settle it by negotiation.
[A party may not serve an ADR notice or commence court proceedings/an arbitration until [21] days after it has made a written offer to the other party(ies) to negotiate a settlement to the dispute.]

It is unlikely that this provision (even if it includes the second sentence) is legally enforceable (see comments in para.2). It is also unlikely that it is effective in practice if one of the parties has no interest in settling the dispute. The argument for including it is that it provides a credible reason for one party approaching another in circumstances where otherwise that party might be concerned that such an approach would be interpreted as a sign of weakness. The counter-argument is that a sensible businessman would not be deterred from opening negotiations by such a concern and that this clause is unnecessary.

The wording in the square brackets is to try and make negotiations obligatory in the sense that it operates as a temporary stay on ADR and court proceedings/arbitration.

MEDIATION

CORE WORDING

2. If any dispute arises out of this agreement, the parties will attempt to settle it by mediation in accordance with the Centre for Dispute Resolution (CEDR) Model Mediation Procedure[("the Model Procedure")].

This clause by itself should be sufficient to give the parties the opportunity to attempt to settle any dispute by mediation/an executive tribunal (see para. 12). The Model Procedure provides clear guidelines on the conduct of the mediation and requires the parties to enter into an agreement based on the Model Mediation Agreement in relation to its conduct. This will deal with points such as the nature of the dispute, the identity of the mediator and where and when the mediation is to take place. There may however be advantages in including at least some of the optional/additional wording (particularly para. 3).

It may be argued that such a clause is an agreement to negotiate in good faith and lacks the necessary certainty to be enforceable. The counter-argument is that an ADR/mediation clause, if it is sufficiently certain and clear as to the process to be used, is enforceable. The reference in the clause to a model procedure may give it that necessary certainty. Additional certainty would be given by the inclusion of the wording in para. 6 below.

This issue is, however, of little practical relevance. The essence of ADR is that it is a consensual process and that parties cannot be forced to resolve their disputes. Most model ADR procedures/rules (see eg CEDR Model Mediation Procedure para. 14) enable a party to terminate a mediation at any time (see however para. 8 below).

The reason for including an ADR clause is essentially the same as for including a negotiation clause (see para. 1 above). The advantage, however, of an ADR clause over a negotiation clause is that:

- *it prompts the parties to consider a process which, unlike negotiation, would not necessarily occur to them:*
- *it introduces a specific process which gives the parties a framework for exploring settlement:*
- *ADR has other advantages over a typical negotiation (see guidance note to Model Procedure).*

If para. 1 (negotiation) has been included this wording needs to be revised so as to read "If the parties are unable to settle any dispute by negotiation [within [21] days] the parties will..."

OPTIONAL/ADDITIONAL WORDING

Triggering/initiating the mediation

3. To initiate a mediation a party [by its Managing Director/...] must give notice in writing ("ADR notice") to the other party(ies) to the dispute [addressed to its/their respective Managing Director/...] requesting a mediation in accordance with clause 2. [A copy of the request should be sent to CEDR.]

This wording is not essential but is recommended. It sets out what is to be done to initiate the mediation provided for in the core wording. As such, it should make it more straightforward for the parties to get the mediation off the ground. In some cases, that may mean the difference between a mediation and no mediation.

The main agreement may have a provision as to how notices are to be served. If not (or even possibly notwithstanding) there may be an advantage in the ADR notice coming from, and being addressed to, a relatively senior executive.

Copying the notice to CEDR will enable CEDR to start administering the process as quickly as possible, and to provide early advice to the parties where appropriate.

Amendments to Model Procedure

4. The procedure in the Model Procedure will be amended to take account of

- any relevant provisions in this agreement;
- any other additional agreement which the parties may enter into in relation to the conduct of the mediation ("Mediation Agreement")

This wording provides for the Model Procedure to be adapted to:
- *any specific wording in the ADR contract clause(s) (see e.g. para. 7.1); and*
- *whatever is agreed in the Mediation Agreement*

Apart from making the position clear, from a legal viewpoint this wording adds further certainty about the process (see commentary on para. 2).

Disagreements on Mediation Agreement

5. If there is any point on the conduct of the mediation (including as to the nomination of the mediator) upon which the parties cannot agree within [14] days from the date of the [ADR notice], CEDR will, at the request of any party, decide that point for the parties, having consulted with them.

This wording almost mirrors paragraph 7 of the Model Procedure. It provides for a specific time from which CEDR can take decision and its inclusion in the contract may reinforce the point that mediation is not to be used as a delaying tactic. (The Model Procedure however does not stop a party commencing or continuing court proceedings/an arbitration.)

This wording should help to speed up the commencement of the mediation by enabling an independent body to decide points upon which the parties can not agree. That body does not have to be CEDR but there are obvious advantages in it being so if CEDR is administering the mediation.

It may also, by providing a mechanism to reduce the uncertainty as to the process, add weight to the argument that the ADR clause is enforceable (see commentary on para. 2).

Timing of mediation

6. The mediation will start not later than [28] days after the date of the ADR notice.

This wording is specifically addressed to the concern that any mediation should provide a quick solution. Without the wording in para. 5 above, it would in practice be difficult to enforce. The wording in para. 5 may, however, by itself be sufficient in that a party could refuse to agree to a late date for the mediation and CEDR is likely to decide on a date which does not involve too much delay.

The best reason for including such wording may be simply that it evidences an intention that any mediation should happen quickly.

JUXTAPOSITION WITH LITIGATION/ARBITRATION

Court proceedings in parallel

7.1 The commencement of a mediation will not prevent the parties commencing or continuing court proceedings/an arbitration.

Strictly this wording is not necessary as nothing in the mediation wording (para. 2) prevents court proceedings. Furthermore paragraph 15 of the Model

Procedure states "Any litigation or arbitration... may be commenced or continued... unless the parties agree otherwise". The inclusion of this wording in the contract clause may however allay the concerns of a party who wishes to retain the ability to resort to court proceedings.

Mediation in parallel

7.2 Any party which commences court proceedings/an arbitration must institute a mediation/serve an ADR notice on the other party(ies) to the court proceedings/arbitration within [21] days.

This wording, which can be used with or without the wording in para. 7.1. is to provide for the situation where the parties wish to retain the ability to go to court but want to add force to the agreement to mediate by requiring the plaintiff party to take steps to institute the mediation within a specified time.

The defendant party can in any event initiate the mediation (eg by serving an ADR notice) at any time.

Unless wording along the lines of para. 7.3 (stay of litigation/arbitration) is included the court proceedings can continue in parallel. If however a stay is provided for, then the plaintiff party will still have time to seek interim relief before serving the ADR notice.

Mediation before litigation

7.3 No party may commence any court proceedings/arbitration in relation to any dispute arising out of this agreement until they have attempted to settle it by mediation and that mediation has terminated.

The rationale for this wording is that an ADR contract clause is intended to curtail court proceedings, etc. and that for them to be run in parallel is not conducive to an attempt to settle. The prospects of settlement may be higher before the lines of battle have been drawn by the hostile step of commencing court proceedings/arbitration:

This wording is the "agreement otherwise" of paragraph 15 of the Model Procedure (see commentary on para. 7.1 above). If a party commences court proceedings/arbitration before attempting mediation it would be open to the other party(ies) to seek a stay pending the mediation.

If a party is concerned that the mediation is being used as a tactic to delay the commencement of court proceedings, it can (unless para. 8 wording has been included) withdraw from the mediation and thereby terminate it (see para. 14 of Model Procedure).

Stay of litigation after interim legal remedies

7.4 Any party which commences court proceedings must institute a mediation/serve an ADR notice on the other party(ies) within [3] days or as soon as an order for interim relief has been made whichever is later. The parties will take no further steps in the court proceedings until the mediation has terminated.

This clause provides for recourse to court proceedings only insofar as is necessary to obtain interim legal remedies eg an interim injunction.

If this wording is not included in the contract clause the parties can still agree to this course of action when a dispute is referred to mediation.

Specific terms may need to be included in this clause or at the time of the stay about the effect of such a stay on time limits in the litigation/arbitration.

OBLIGATORY MEDIATION – RESTRICTION ON TERMINATION

8. Neither party may terminate the mediation until each party has made its opening presentation and the mediator has met each party separately for at least [one hour]. Thereafter paragraph 14 of the Model Procedure will apply.

Paragraph 14 of the Model Procedure states that "Any of the Parties may terminate the [ADR] at any time...". It would therefore be open to a party to negate the intent of the core wording by withdrawing from the mediation as soon as it starts (see para. 2 above). Experience shows, however, that a skillful neutral/mediator may be able to increase the possibilities of a settlement if he/she is given the opportunity. The purpose of this wording is to give that opportunity, albeit to a limited extent, whilst not seriously undermining the intent of paragraph 14.

EXECUTIVE TRIBUNAL

9. *The wording for an Executive Tribunal (sometimes called a "mini trial") can be easily adapted from the wording for a mediation. In most cases this will simply involve substituting "executive tribunal" for "mediation" (see paras 3–7, 7.1–7.4 & 10). The other changes are:*

PARA NO.	SUBSTITUTE	FOR
2	Model Executive Tribunal Procedure	Model Mediation Procedure
4	an Executive Tribunal Agreement	a Mediation Agreement
8	Neither party may terminate the executive tribunal until each party has made its opening presentation and the neutral and the executives have met together for at least [1] hour. Thereafter para. 15 of the Model Procedure will apply."	[The wording in para. 8]

There may also be consequential amendments to the cross references to the para. no's in the Model Executive Tribunal Procedure.

ARBITRATION

10. If the parties have not settled the dispute by the mediation within [42] days from when the mediation was instituted/the date of the ADR notice, the dispute shall [be referred to, and finally resolved by, arbitration under the Rules of the London Court of International Arbitration/Chartered Institute of Arbitrators/[relevant arbitral body] which Rules are deemed to be incorporated by reference to this clause.]

If the parties to the agreement want the ultimate method of resolving any dispute to be arbitration rather than litigation/court proceedings, wording along these lines should be included. If no wording along the lines of para. 7.1 or 7.3 has been included then strictly a straight arbitration clause, without the reference to mediation, would suffice.

The arbitration reference wording used should be the model/recommended wording of the arbitral body to which the reference is to be made (or whose rules are to be used).

If the "core" ADR/mediation clause does not include provision for service of an ADR notice (see para. 3 above) the wording should be amended to refer to the "initiation of the mediation" (although there is scope for dispute as to when initiation occurs, which is one reason why the wording in para. 3 is recommended).

LITIGATION

11. *If the parties to the agreement want the ultimate method of resolving any dispute to be court proceedings, rather than arbitration, there is no need for any additional wording to provide for this (although choice of law and jurisdiction clauses may need to be included).*

© CEDR

The Chartered Institute of Arbitrators

GUIDELINES FOR CONCILIATION AND MEDIATION (1990)

1. *Application of these Guidelines*

1.1 Conciliation or mediation are available to parties who have a dispute or difference arising out of a contract or some other legal relationship and who wish to resolve their dispute or difference amicably without recourse to the procedures of litigation or arbitration.

1.2 The parties may use the Conciliation and Mediation Service of the Chartered Institute of Arbitrators if they have agreed in writing to submit their dispute or difference for resolution under these Guidelines

1.3 The parties may, by agreement, adapt these Guidelines to suit their particular purposes.

2. *Commencement of Conciliation or Mediation Proceedings*

2.1 The parties should submit a joint application in writing to the Chartered Institute on the prescribed form, accompanied by the appropriate registration fee.

2.2 The parties should state clearly in the application form whether they require conciliation or mediation. This is because the conciliator will not normally make recommendations for the determination of the dispute (although he/she may if the parties call upon him/her to do so or if he/she considers it appropriate to do so and the parties agree), whereas the mediator will in every case make recommendations.

2.3 The application form requires the entry of only basic information, such as the names and addresses of the parties, address for service of documents (if different) and brief particulars of the dispute or difference. A copy of the relevant contract should (where applicable) also be attached.

2.4 Conciliation or mediation proceedings will be confidential and privileged. For the purposes of the law of evidence, therefore, none of the following parties may be called upon or compelled by a subpoena to give evidence of the conciliation or mediation proceedings in any connected arbitration or litigation proceedings or to disclose any matters arising from the conciliation or mediation proceedings to any third parties who are interested in or connected with the dispute or difference:

i.   The conciliator or mediator;
ii. A party;
iii. Any expert or legal adviser of the conciliator or mediator;
iv. Any expert or legal adviser of a party;
v.   Any witness for a party, whether an expert witness or a witness as to fact.

The parties to the conciliation or mediation must serve notice to this effect on any third parties, accompanied by a copy of these Guidelines and of the application for conciliation or mediation.

3.   Appointment of a Conciliator or Mediator

3.1   Where the Chartered Institute is satisfied with the validity of the parties' application, it will appoint a conciliator or mediator. Although account will be taken of representations made by the parties as to the qualifications and/or identity of the appointee, all appointments will be in the exclusive and unfettered control of the Chartered Institute.

3.2   Proceedings will normally be conducted by a single conciliator or mediator but:

i.   The parties may each appoint one conciliator or mediator. If the two conciliators or mediators consider it appropriate, they may request the Chartered Institute to appoint a third conciliator or mediator.
ii. If a third conciliator or mediator is appointed, his/her fees and expenses will be borne jointly by the parties.

3.3   The Chartered Institute reserves the right to appoint a substitute conciliator or mediator on the application of either party where the original appointee dies, or becomes incapacitated, or fails to proceed with reasonable dispatch or is for any reason disqualified from or incapable of proceeding.

4.   Procedure

4.1   The conciliator or mediator will act in an independent, impartial and just manner. The procedure is intended to assist the parties to reach an amicable and equitable settlement of their dispute or difference, and so the conciliator or mediator may conduct the proceedings in such manner as he/she considers appropriate and will take particular account of the following matters:

i.   The general circumstances of the case;
ii.   The business relationship of the parties;
iii. The parties' wishes;
iv.   The need for a speedy and economical settlement;
v.   Whether the matter may be disposed of by the use of a documents-only procedure.

4.2   The conciliator or mediator will fix time limits within which the parties' statements of case, statement of agreed facts, relevant documents and other evidence should be submitted to him/her and between themselves. He/she will also fix time limits for statements of reply and for such other steps as he/she may require. He/she will, however, have a discretion as to the procedure for exchanging cases.

4.3   The conciliator will also have the following powers:

i.   To require the submission of further evidence and/or information;
ii.   To require the submission of further statements of case and reply;
iii. To require the furnishing of samples in sale and supply of goods cases;
iv.   To carry out a site visit;
v.   To convene an informal hearing and examine the parties and any witnesses orally;
vi.   To interview the parties separately;
vii. To seek legal or expert technical advice;
viii. To require the parties to provide security for his/her costs.

4.4   Where factual information is given or allegations made by a party to the conciliation or mediator in separate interviews, such information or allegations may be disclosed to the other party for comment, but only with the consent of the disclosing party.

4.5   The conciliator or mediator will use his/her best endeavours to commence the conciliation or mediation as soon as possible after appointment and to conclude it within three months of commencement. The parties may, however, agree to an extension of time for this.

5.   *Settlement of Disputes or Differences*

5.1   At any stage in the proceedings, the conciliator or mediator may express a preliminary view on the dispute or difference referred to him/her and the parties may submit to him/her their own proposals for settlement.

5.2   A conciliator may, and a mediator will, submit his/her proposals for settlement to the parties for comment. Proposals will be resubmitted by the conciliator or mediator after he/she has taken account of the parties' comments. The initial proposals will normally be submitted within 21 days of the conclusion of an informal hearing, a site visit or receipt by the conciliator or mediator of legal or expert opinion.

5.3   Where a settlement is reached, whether by the parties themselves or through the good offices of the conciliator or mediator, the parties should draw up a settlement agreement or request the conciliator or mediator to do so. This agreement, when signed, and witnessed by the conciliator or mediator, will give the settlement contractual effect and thus will be legally binding. The contents of the agreement will be confidential and may not be disclosed by a party except for the purpose of enforcing it in legal proceedings

5.4   It is strongly recommended that parties should embody the terms of settlement in a settlement agreement because the agreement will provide written evidence of the settlement in the event of a further dispute or if enforcement through the courts becomes necessary.

6.   *Termination of Conciliation or Mediation Proceedings*

6.1   Conciliation or mediation proceedings may be concluded at any time by:

i.   Withdrawal from the proceedings following the giving of written notice by one party to the other;

ii.   Written notice from both parties to the conciliator or mediator;

iii.   Written notice from the conciliator or mediator to the parties stating that continued attempts to conciliate or mediate are no longer justified;

iv.   The making of a settlement agreement;

v.   The issue of legal or arbitral proceedings on the same subject-matter, except for protective applications.

7.   *Legal or Arbitral Proceedings after Conciliation or Mediation*

7.1   Once the conciliation or mediation proceedings have been brought to an end, the parties may refer to arbitration or to litigation:

i.   Any question which has not been settled by conciliation or mediation proceedings;

ii.   Any question arising out of or in connection with a settlement agreement, including enforcement.

7.2   Because of the differing rules of evidence relating to conciliation and mediation on the one hand and arbitration or litigation on the other, the conciliator or mediator may not, unless the parties otherwise agree, act as arbitrator, advocate, representative or witness in any arbitration or litigation proceedings arising from or connected with the subject-matter of the conciliation or mediation proceedings.

7.3   Likewise, because of the application of the legal rules of evidence, neither the parties nor their witnesses nor their advisers may refer to any of the following matters in any legal or arbitral proceedings (whether or not arising from or connected with the subject-matter of the conciliation or mediation proceedings):

i.   Views expressed or suggestions made by either party or the conciliator or mediator in connection with a possible settlement of the whole or any part of the dispute or difference;

ii.   Admissions made by either party during the conciliation or mediation proceedings;

iii.   Proposals made by the conciliator or mediator;

iv.   The parties' replies to proposals made by the conciliator or mediator, whether expressed in open or 'without prejudice' correspondence or other documents;

v.   Evidence of abortive draft settlement agreements.

8.   *Costs*

8.1   Unless the parties agree otherwise in a settlement agreement, the costs of the conciliation or mediation proceedings will be borne equally between them. These costs include:

i.   The reasonable fees of the conciliator or mediator, whether or not a settlement is reached;

ii.   The travel and other out-of-pocket expenses of the conciliator or mediator;

iii.   The cost of any legal or expert technical advice requested by the conciliator or mediator;

iv.   Where the parties each appoint a conciliator or mediator, the reasonable fees and travel and other out-of-pocket expenses of a third conciliator or mediator;

v.   The cost of arranging for site visits or the examination of samples;

vi.   The Chartered Institute's administrative charges, including the cost of providing any services required of it.

8.2   The parties will bear their own costs of preparing and submitting their cases to conciliation or mediation. These costs include such items as hire of a venue for an informal hearing, the travel and out-of-pocket expenses of the parties' witnesses and legal or technical advice.

8.3   At the start of the proceedings, the conciliator or mediator may require each party to deposit an equal amount as an advance towards the costs of the conciliation or mediation proceedings defined in article 8.1 above. He/she may also require supplementary deposits as the proceedings progress. Monies left over at the end of the proceedings from any deposits received will be refunded to the parties in equal amounts. Alternatively, the conciliator or mediator may require the parties to give security for these costs.

8.4   Where the conciliator or mediator orders the payment of deposits or the giving of security for costs, he/she may, by written notice to the parties, suspend or terminate the proceedings if his/her order is not complied with.

The Chartered Institute of Arbitrators

Conciliation and Mediation Service

Application for Conciliation or Mediation

1. . . . . .First Party
   of . . . . .Tel: . . . .

and

. . . . .Second Party
of Tel: . . . .

hereby apply to the Chartered Institute of Arbitrators for the following dispute to be referred to conciliation/mediation* under the Guidelines for Conciliation and Mediation.

2. The dispute has arisen in connection with the following:

   . . . .
   . . . .
   . . . .
   . . . .
   . . . .

   NOTE: Only an outline is required here to enable the dispute to be identified by the parties and the Institute.

   *Delete as appropriate

3. A cheque for £86.25 inclusive of VAT (payable to the Chartered Institute of Arbitrators) in respect of the Institute's registration/appointment fee is enclosed .

   SIGNED:

   . . . . .Date . . . .
   (First Party)

   . . . . .Date . . . .
   (Second Party)

Chartered Institute of Arbitrators,
75 Cannon Street,   Tel: 071 236 8761
London, EC4N 5BH   Fax: 071 236 5204

© Chartered Institute of Arbitrators

NB Fee details and contact address have changed from those set out in the printed form

Centre for Dispute Resolution: Model Mediation Procedure
including guidance notes (1996)

Model Mediation Procedure

Mediation Procedure

1. The Parties to the Dispute or negotiation in question will attempt to settle it by mediation. Representatives of the Parties [and their Advisers] and the Mediator[s] will attend [a] Mediation meetings[s]. All communications relating to, and at, the Mediation will be without prejudice.

2. The Representatives must have the necessary authority to settle the Dispute. The procedure at the Mediation will be determined by the Mediator, after consultation with the Representatives.

Mediation Agreement

3. The Parties, the Mediator and CEDR will enter into an agreement ("Mediation Agreement") based on the CEDR Model Mediation Agreement ("the Model Agreement") in relation to the conduct of the Mediation.

The Mediator

4. The Mediator will:

- attend any meetings with any or all of the Parties preceding the Mediation, if requested or if the Mediator decides this is appropriate;
- read before the Mediation each Summary and all the Documents sent to him/her in accordance with paragraph 9;
- determine the procedure (see paragraph 2 above);
- assist the parties in drawing up any written settlement agreement;
- abide by the terms of the Model Procedure, the Mediation Agreement and CEDR's Code of Conduct.

5. The Mediator [and any member of the Mediator's firm or company] will not act for any of the Parties individually in connection with the Dispute in any capacity either during the currency of this agreement or at any time thereafter. The Parties accept that in relation to the Dispute neither the Mediator nor CEDR is an agent of, or acting in any capacity for, any of the

Parties. The Parties and the Mediator accept that the Mediator (unless an employee of CEDR) is acting as an independent contractor and not as agent or employee of CEDR.

CEDR

6. CEDR, in conjunction with the Mediator, will make the necessary arrangements for the Mediation including, as necessary:

- assisting the Parties in appointing the Mediator and in drawing up the Mediation Agreement;
- organising a suitable venue and dates;
- organising exchange of the Summaries and Documents;
- meeting with any or all of the Representatives (and the Mediator if he/she has been appointed) either together or separately, to discuss any matters or concerns relating to the Mediation;
- general administration in relation to the Mediation.

7. If a dispute is referred to CEDR as a result of a mediation (or other ADR) clause in a contract, and if there is any issue with regard to the conduct of the Mediation (including as to the appointment of the Mediator) upon which the Parties cannot agree within a reasonable time from the date of the notice initiating the Mediation ("the ADR notice") CEDR will, at the request of any Party, decide the issue for the Parties, having consulted with them.

Other participants

8. Each Party will notify the other party[ies], through CEDR, of the names of those people (the Adviser[s], witnesses etc – in addition to the Representatives) that it intends will be present on its behalf at the Mediation. Each Party, in signing the Mediation Agreement, will be deemed to be agreeing on behalf of both itself and all such persons to be bound by the confidentiality provisions of this Model Procedure.

Exchange of information

9. Each Party will, simultaneously through CEDR, exchange with the other and send to the Mediator at least two weeks before the Mediation or such other date as may be agreed between the Parties:

- a concise summary ("the Summary") stating its case in the Dispute;
- copies of all the documents to which it refers in the Summary and to which it may want to refer in the Mediation ("the Documents").

In addition, each Party may send to the Mediator (through CEDR) and/or bring to the Mediation further documentation which it wishes to disclose in confidence to the Mediator but not to any other Party, clearly stating in writing that such documentation is confidential to the Mediator and CEDR.

10. The Parties will, through CEDR, agree the maximum number of pages of each Summary and of the Documents and try to agree a joint set of documents from their respective Documents.

The Mediation

11. No formal record or transcript of the Mediation will be made.

12. If the Parties are unable to reach a settlement in the negotiations at the Mediation and only if all the Representatives so request and the Mediator agrees, the Mediator will produce for the Parties a non-binding written recommendation on terms of settlement. This will not attempt to anticipate what a court might order but will set out what the Mediator suggests are appropriate settlement terms in all of the circumstances.

Settlement agreement

13. Any settlement reached in the Mediation will not be legally binding until it has been reduced to writing and signed by, or on behalf of, the Parties.

Termination

14. Any of the Parties may withdraw from the Mediation at any time and shall immediately inform the Mediator and the other Representatives in writing. The Mediation will terminate when:

- a Party withdraws from the Mediation; or
- a written settlement agreement is concluded; or
- the Mediator decides that continuing the Mediation is unlikely to result in a settlement; or
- the Mediator decides he should retire for any of the reasons in the Code of Conduct.

Stay of proceedings

15. Any litigation or arbitration in relation to the Dispute may be commenced or continued notwithstanding the Mediation unless the Parties agree otherwise.

Confidentiality etc

16. Every person involved in the Mediation will keep confidential and not use for any collateral or ulterior purpose:

- the fact that the Mediation is to take place or has taken place; and
- all information, (whether given orally, in writing or otherwise), produced for, or arising in relation to, the Mediation including the settlement agreement (if any) arising out of it

except insofar as is necessary to implement and enforce any such settlement agreement.

17. All documents (which includes anything upon which evidence is recorded including tapes and computer discs) or other information produced for, or arising in relation to, the Mediation will be privileged and not be admissible as evidence or discoverable in any litigation or arbitration connected with the Dispute except any documents or other information which would in any event have been admissible or discoverable in any such litigation or arbitration.

18. None of the parties to the Mediation Agreement will call the Mediator or CEDR (or any employee, consultant, officer or representative of CEDR) as a witness, consultant, arbitrator or expert in any litigation or arbitration in relation to the Dispute and the Mediator and CEDR will not voluntarily act in any such capacity without the written agreement of all the Parties.

Fees, expenses and costs

19. CEDR's fees (which include the Mediator's fees) and the other expenses of the Mediation will be borne equally by the Parties. Payment of these fees and expenses will be made to CEDR in accordance with its fee schedule and terms and conditions of business.

20. Each Party will bear its own costs and expenses of its participation in the Mediation.

Waiver of liability

21. Neither the Mediator nor CEDR shall be liable to the Parties for any act or omission in connection with the services provided by them in, or in relation to, the Mediation, unless the act or omission is fraudulent or involves wilful misconduct.

Guidance notes

The paragraph numbers and headings in these notes refer to the paragraphs and headings in the Model Procedure

Text in the Model Procedure in square brackets may be inappropriate and therefore inapplicable in some cases.

Introduction

The essence of mediation (and many other ADR procedures) is that:

- it involves a neutral third party to facilitate negotiations;
- it is quick, inexpensive and confidential;
- it enables the parties to reach results which are not possible in an adjudicative process such as litigation or arbitration and may be to the benefit of both parties, particularly if there is a continuing business relationship;

- it involves representatives of the parties who have sufficient authority to settle. In some cases, there may be an advantage in the representatives being people who have not been directly involved in the events leading up to the dispute and in the subsequent dispute.

The procedure for the mediation is flexible and this model procedure can be adapted (with or without the assistance of CEDR) to suit the parties. A mediation can be used:

- in both domestic and international disputes
- whether or not litigation or arbitration has been commenced; and
- in two party and multi-party disputes.

Rules or rigid procedures in the context of a consensual and adaptable process which is the essence of ADR are generally inappropriate. The Model Procedure and the Model Agreement and these guidance notes should be sufficient to enable parties to conduct a mediation.

In some cases the agreement to conduct a mediation will be as a result of an "ADR clause" (such as one of the CEDR Model ADR clauses) to that effect in an underlying commercial agreement between the Parties. Where that is the case the Model Procedure and Mediation Agreement may need to be adapted accordingly.

The Model Agreement, which has been kept as short and simple as possible, incorporates the Model Procedure (see para. 3).The Mediation Agreement can include amendments to the Model Procedure; the amendments can be set out in the body of the Mediation Agreement or the Mediation Agreement can state that amendments made in manuscript (or otherwise) to the Model Procedure and initialled by the Parties are to be incorporated into the Mediation Agreement.

Mediation Procedure – paras 1 and 2

The Advisers, can and usually do attend the Mediation. Although a lead role in the Mediation is often taken by the Representatives, the Advisers can play an important role in the exchange of information, in advising their clients on the legal implications of a settlement and in drawing up the settlement agreement. However, the commercial interests of the Parties will normally take the negotiations beyond strict legal issues, hence the importance of the role of the Representatives.

It is essential that the Representatives are sufficiently senior and have the authority of their respective Parties to settle the Dispute.

Mediation Agreement– para 3

If CEDR is asked to do so by a party wishing to initiate a mediation, it will approach the other party(ies) to a dispute to seek to persuade it/them to participate.

Ideally the Representatives, the Advisers (and the Mediator if he/she has been identified) and CEDR (or whatever other ADR body is involved, if any) should meet to discuss and finalise the terms of the Mediation Agreement.

Alternatively, the party who has taken the initiative in proposing the Mediation may wish to send a draft agreement based on the CEDR Model Mediation Agreement to the other party(ies).

The Mediator – paras 4–5

The success of the Mediation will, to a large extent, depend on the skill of the Mediator. CEDR believes it is very important for the Mediator to have had specific training and experience. CEDR has its own body of trained and experienced mediators and can assist the Parties in identifying a suitable mediator.

In some cases it may be useful to have more than one Mediator, or to have an independent expert who can advise the Mediator on technical issues ("the Mediator's Adviser"). All should sign the Mediation Agreement which should be amended as appropriate.

It is CEDR's practice, as part of its mediator training programme, to have a pupil mediator ("the Pupil Mediator") attend most mediations. The Pupil Mediator signs the Mediation Agreement and falls within the definition "the Mediator" in the Model Procedure and the Mediation Agreement.

It is advisable, but not essential, to involve the Mediator in any preliminary meeting between the Parties.

CEDR – paras 6–7

The Code of Conduct covers such points as the Mediator's duty of confidentiality, impartiality and avoiding cotlflicts of interest.

The Model Procedure envisages the involvement of CEDR because in most cases this is likely to benefit the Parties and generally to facilitate the setting up and conduct of the Mediation. Its involvement, however, is not essential and this Model Procedure can be amended if CEDR is not to be involved.

Exchange of information – paras 9–10

Documentation which a Party wants the Mediator to keep confidential from the other Party(ies) (e.g. a counsel's opinion, an expert report not yet exchanged) must be clearly marked as such. It can be disclosed by the Party before or during the Mediation. It will not be disclosed by the Mediator or CEDR without the express consent of the Party.

One of the advantages of ADR is that it can avoid the excessive discovery process (including witness statements) which often blights litigation and arbitration. The Documents should be kept to the minimum necessary to give the Mediator a good grasp of the issues. The Summaries should be similarly brief.

The Mediation – paras 11–12

The intention of paragraph 12 is that the Mediator will cease to play an entirely facilitative role only if the negotiations in the Mediation are deadlocked. Giving a settlement recommendation may be perceived by a Party as undermining the Mediator's neutrality and for this reason the Mediator may not agree to this course of action. Any recommendation will be without prejudice and will not be binding.

Settlement agreement – para 13

If no agreement is reached, it is nonetheless open to the Parties to adjourn the Mediation to another time and place. Experience shows that even where no agreement is reached during mediation itself, the Parties will often reach a settlement shortly after, as a result of the progress made during that mediation.

Stay of proceedings – para 15

Although a stay may engender a better climate for settlement, it is not however essential that any proceedings relating to the Dispute should be stayed. If they are stayed, the effect on limitation periods needs to be agreed. Although under English law the parties can agree to limitation periods not running the position may differ in other jurisdictions and the position on this should be checked.

Confidentiality– paras 16–18

The CEDR Code of Conduct provides that the Mediator is not to disclose to any other Party any information given to him by a Party in confidence without the express consent of that Party.

In any related litigation in England and Wales such documents (see paragraph 16) should in any event be inadmissible and privileged as "without prejudice" documents since they will have been produced in relation to negotiations to settle the dispute. Documents which preexisted the Mediation and would in any event have been discoverable will, however, not become privileged by reason of having been referred to in the Mediation and will therefore still be discoverable. The position rnay differ in other jurisdictions and should be checked.

Fees, expenses and costs – paras 19–20

The usual arrangement is for the Parties to share equally the fees and expenses of the procedure, but other arrangments are possible. A party to a dispute which is reluctant to participate in a mediation may be persuaded to participate if the other party(ies) agree to bear that party's share of the mediation fees.

International disputes –Language and governing law/jurisdiction

The Model Agreement is designed for domestic disputes but can be easily adapted for international cross-border disputes by the addition of the following paragraphs:
"Language
The language of the Mediation will be... Any Party producing documents or participating in the Mediation in any other language will provide the necessary translations and interpretation facilities."
"Governing Law and Jurisdiction
The Mediation Agreement shall be governed by, construed and take effect in accordance with [English] law.

The courts of [England] shall have exclusive jurisdiction to settle any claim, dispute or matter of difference which may arise out of or in connection with the Mediation."

Where the law is not English or the jurisdiction not England the Mediation Agreement may need to be amended to ensure the structure, rights and obligations necessary for a mediation are applicable.

© CEDR

CENTRE FOR DISPUTE RESOLUTION

MODEL MEDIATION AGREEMENT

Date
_____

Parties

1: _____ ("Party A") _____

2: _____ ("Party B") _____

[3: _____ ("Party C") etc]

(jointly "the Parties")   Add full names and addresses

[4: _____ ("the Mediator")]

[5: _____ ("the Pupil Mediator") ("the Mediator's Adviser")]

(jointly and individually "the Mediator")

[6] European Dispute Resolution Limited trading as the Centre for Dispute Resolution, 7 St Katharine's Way, London E1 9LB ("CEDR")

Dispute ("the Dispute")

Brief description of the dispute.

Participation in a Mediation

1. The Parties will attempt to settle the Dispute by mediation ("the Mediation"). The provisions of the CEDR Model Mediation Procedure ("the Model Procedure") (a copy of which is attached) as supplemented and/or varied by this agreement will apply to the Mediation and are incorporated in, and form part of, this agreement. The definitions in the Model Procedure are used in this agreement.

The Mediator

2. The Mediator[s] will be _____ [The Pupil Mediator will be   ]

   [The Mediator's Adviser will be _____]

The Representatives

3. The Representatives for the Parties at the Mediation will be:

   Add full names and corporate titles

   Party A: _____

   Party B _____

   [Party C etc: _____]

   (jointly "the Representatives")

   A Party will immediately notify the other Party[ies] and the Mediator of any change to the above.

NB CEDR address has now changed

Other participants

4. The following, in addition to the Representatives, will be present on behalf of the Parties at the Mediation

Party A: _____

Party B: _____

[Party C   ]

A Party will immediately notify the other Party(ies) and the Mediator of any change to the above.

Place and time

5. The Mediation will take place

at: _____

on: _____

starting at: _____ o'clock

Confidentiality

6. Each Representative in signing this agreement is deemed to be agreeing to the confidentiality provisions of the Model Procedure (paras 16–17) on behalf of the Party he/she represents and all other persons present on behalf of that Party at the Mediation.

Litigation/arbitration

7. No litigation or arbitration in relation to the Dispute is to be commenced [Any existing litigation or arbitration in relation to the Dispute is to be stayed] from the date of this agreement until the termination of the Mediation.

This paragraph is only necessary if there is to be a restriction on litigation/arbitration – see para 15 of Model Procedure.

Model Procedure amendments

8. *Set out amendments (if any) to the Model Procedure – see introduction to Model Procedure guidance notes.*

Law and jurisdiction

9. *For wording see Model Procedure guidance notes . This paragraph only necessary if the Dispute involves parties from different jurisdictions.*

Signed: _____

on behalf of [Party A] _____

Signed: _____

on behalf of [Party B] [Party C] _____

Signed: _____

[the Mediator] [[the Pupil Mediator] [the Mediator's Adviser] _____

Signed: _____

on behalf of CEDR _____

© CEDR

The Institution of Civil Engineers: Conciliation Procedure (1994)

1   This Procedure shall apply whenever
   (a) the Parties have entered into a contract which provides for Conciliation for any dispute which may arise between the Parties in accordance with the Institution of Civil Engineers' Conciliation Procedure, or
   (b) where the Parties have agreed that the Institution of Civil Engineers' Conciliation Procedure shall apply.

2   This Procedure shall be interpreted and applied in the manner most conducive to the efficient conduct of the proceedings with the primary objective of achieving a settlement to the dispute by agreement between the Parties as quickly as possible.

3   Subject to the provision of the Contract relating to Conciliation, any Party to the Contract may by giving to the other Party a written notice, hereafter called a Notice of Conciliation, request that any dispute in connection with or arising out of the Contract or the carrying out of the Works shall be referred to a Conciliator. Such Notice shall be accompanied by a brief statement of the matter which it is desired to refer to Conciliation, and the relief or remedy sought.

4   Save where a Conciliator has already been appointed, the Parties shall agree upon a Conciliator within 14 days of the Notice being given under Paragraph 3. In default of agreement any Party may request the President (or, if he is unable to act, any Vice President) for the time being of the Institution of Civil Engineers to appoint a Conciliator within 14 days of receipt of the request by him, which request shall be accompanied by a copy of the Notice of Conciliation.

5   If, for any reason whatsoever, the Conciliator is unable, or fails to complete the Conciliation in accordance with this Procedure, then any Party may require the appointment of a replacement Conciliator in accordance with the procedures of Paragraph 4.

6   The Party requesting Conciliation shall deliver to the Conciliator, immediately on his appointment, and at the same time to the other Party if

this has not already been done, a copy of the Notice of Conciliation, or as otherwise required by the Contract, together with copies of all relevant Notices of Dispute and of any other notice or decision which is a condition precedent to Conciliation.

7   The Conciliator shall start the Conciliation as soon as possible after his appointment and shall use his best endeavours to conclude the Conciliation as soon as possible and in any event within any time limit as may be stated in the Contract, or two months from the date of his appointment, or within such other time as may be agreed between the Parties.

8   Any Party may, upon receipt of notice of the appointment of the Conciliator and within such period as the Conciliator may allow, send to the Conciliator and to the other Party a statement of its views on the dispute and any issues that is considers to be of relevance to the dispute, and any financial consequences.

9   As soon as possible after his appointment, the Conciliator shall issue instructions establishing, inter alia, the date and place for the Conciliation meeting with the Parties. Each Party shall inform the Conciliator in writing of the name of its representative for the Conciliation, who shall have full authority to act on behalf of that Party, and the names of any other persons who will attend the Conciliation meeting. This information shall be given at least seven days before the Conciliation meeting with copies to the other Party.

10   The Conciliator may, entirely at his own discretion, issue such further instructions as he considers to be appropriate, meet and question the Parties and their representatives, together or separately, investigate the facts and circumstances of the dispute, visit the site and request the production of documents or the attendance of people whom he considers could assist in any way. The Conciliator may conduct the proceedings in any way that he wishes, and with the prior agreement of the Parties obtain legal or technical advice, the cost of which shall be met by the Parties, in accordance with Paragraph 17, or as may be agreed by the Parties and the Conciliator.

11   The Conciliator may consider and discuss such solutions to the dispute as he thinks appropriate or as may be suggested by any Party. He shall observe and maintain the confidentiality of particular information which he is given by any Party privately, and may disclose it only with the explicit permission of that Party. He will try to assist the Parties to resolve the dispute in any way which is acceptable to them.

12   Any Party may, at any time, ask that additional claims or disputes, or additional parties, shall be joined in the Conciliation. Such application shall be accompanied by details of the relevant contractual facts, notices and decisions. Such joinder shall be subject to the agreement of the Conciliator

and all other Parties. Any additional party shall, unless otherwise agreed by the Parties, have the same rights and obligations as the other Parties to the Conciliation.

13 If, in the opinion of the Conciliator, the resolution of the dispute would be assisted by further investigation by any Party or by the Conciliator, or by an interim agreement, including some action by any Party, then the Conciliator will, with the agreement of the Parties, give instructions and adjourn the proceedings as may be appropriate.

14 Once a settlement has been achieved of the whole or any part of the matters in dispute, the Conciliator may assist the Parties to prepare an Agreement incorporating the terms of the settlement.

15 If, in the opinion of the Conciliator, it is unlikely that the Parties will achieve an agreed settlement to their disputes, or if any Party fails to respond to an instruction by the Conciliator, or upon the request of any Party, the Conciliator may advise all Parties accordingly and will forthwith prepare his Recommendation.

16 The Conciliator's Recommendation shall state his solution to the dispute which has been referred for Conciliation. The Recommendation shall not disclose any information which any Party has provided in confidence. It shall be based on his opinion as to how the Parties can best dispose of the dispute between them and need not necessarily be based on any principles of the Contract, law, or equity. The Conciliator shall not be required to give reasons for his Recommendation. Nevertheless, should he choose to do so, his reasons shall be issued as a separate document, within 7 days of the giving of his Recommendation.

17 When a settlement has been reached or when the Conciliator has prepared his Recommendation, or at an earlier date solely at the discretion of the Conciliator, he shall notify the Parties in writing and send them an account of his fees and disbursements. Unless otherwise agreed between themselves each Party shall be responsible for paying and shall within 7 days of receipt of the account from the Conciliator pay an equal share save that the Parties shall be jointly and severally liable to the Conciliator for the whole of his account. Upon receipt of payment in full the Conciliator shall send his Recommendation to all the Parties. If any Party fails to make the payment due from him the other Party may pay the sum to the Conciliator and recover the amount from the defaulting Party as a debt due. Each Party shall meet his own costs and expenses.

18 The Conciliator may be recalled, by written agreement of the Parties and upon payment of an additional fee, to clarify, amplify or give further consideration to any provision of the Recommendation.

19 The Conciliator shall not be appointed arbitrator in any subsequent arbitration between the Parties whether arising out of the dispute, difference or other matter or otherwise arising out of the same Contract unless the Parties otherwise agree in writing. No Party shall be entitled to call the Conciliator as a witness in any subsequent arbitration or litigation concerning the subject matter of the Conciliation.

20 The confidential nature of the Conciliation shall be respected by every person who in involved in whatever capacity.

21 The Conciliator shall not be liable to the Parties or any person claiming through them for any matter arising out of or in connection with the Conciliation or the way in which it is or has been concluded, and the Parties will not themselves bring any such claims against him.

22 Any notice required under this Procedure shall be sent to the Parties by recorded delivery to the principal place of business or if a company to its registered office, or to the address which the Party has notified to the Conciliator. Any notice required by this Procedure to be sent to the Conciliator shall be sent by recorded delivery to him a the address which he shall notify to the Parties on his appointment.

23 In this Procedure where the context so requires 'Party' shall mean 'Parties' and 'he' shall mean 'she'.

© Institution of Civil Engineers, London

The Chartered Institute of Arbitrators: Guidelines for Supervised Settlement Procedure ('Mini-Trial') (1990)

Explanatory Notes

Introduction

Most bona fide disputes between reputable parties are capable of settlement in a manner that is business oriented, thus avoiding or at least curtailing legal expenditure, the loss of executive time and the deterioration of valuable business relationships.

Such a settlement can be facilitated by the use of a structured procedure which ensures that authorised management representatives are presented with the facts, viewed from both sides, and can then enter into negotiations under the guidance of a neutral adviser experienced in conciliation, mediation and arbitration techniques.

The procedure can be invoked at an early stage when there is goodwill and a history of good relationships or after litigation or arbitration has been initiated.

Preliminary

There should be a preliminary investigation of the facts, documentation and expert and other testimony, sufficient to enable the parties to be appraised of the situation by their advisers.

The Procedure

1. *The Initiating Agreement (form attached below):*

   (a) Senior management representatives with authority to negotiate and arrive at a settlement (even if subject to board ratification) should be identified and appointed by both sides. They can be assisted by inhouse or outside legal advisers but should not be accompanied by more than one person at the formal meeting. If possible, it is better that the management representatives to be appointed should not be the persons involved in the events that brought about the disputes (who might have a personal stake in the outcome).

(b) The parties will agree upon and appoint (or ask the Chartered Institute of Arbitrators to appoint) a neutral adviser who will have the same qualities of impartiality and lack of bias as would be required of an arbitrator. His fee will be established and agreed at the time of the appointment. There will be no unilateral communication with the neutral adviser prior to the formal meeting, except for the purposes of appointment.

(c) The parties will agree the form of and sign the initiating agreement. In an international case, they will agree the law to apply, the language of the meeting and of the documentation and, where necessary, see that appropriate translations of the documents into the agreed language are available, together with interpreters etc.

2. *Exchange of Information*

By a date laid down in the initiating agreement, the parties will exchange, and submit also to the neutral adviser, concise statements setting out the issues and their respective positions as regards the issues and, where appropriate, will add an estimate of their likely claims in financial terms. They will exchange copies of letters, documents and exhibits and expert reports upon which they intend to rely at the formal meeting, or which they consider helpful in explaining their position. Only material that can have an important and direct bearing on the issues should be produced.

3. *The Formal Meeting*

A formal meeting will be held before a panel consisting of the management representatives and the neutral adviser who will conduct the meeting.

Each party, by its appointed advocate (who may or may not be the party's legal adviser or counsel) will make an oral presentation of the case of the party which he represents, referring, where appropriate, to documentation and examining witnesses and experts. There will be no cross-examination but the management representatives and the neutral adviser may ask elucidating questions. Subject to that, the presentations will not be interrrupted. Each side will have a right of reply when the other side has stated its case.

The proceedings will not be recorded, although the parties may take notes.

A time limit for the meeting may be agreed or set.

4. Negotiations

At the conclusion of the formal meeting, the management representatives will discuss and endeavour to agree on a resolution of the dispute. The opinion of the neutral adviser may be sought at, or after, the formal meeting and, by agreement of both sides, he may produce a written report. The meeting, for the purpose of continuing the negotiations, may be adjourned and reconvened as necessary. After the conclusion of the formal meeting, the neutral adviser may act as conciliator or mediator and shuttle between the parties, if so desired, and if a settlement emerges it will be reduced to a written agreement, with or without the assistance of the neutral adviser, and will be signed by the management representatives and witnessed by the neutral adviser. This agreement, once signed, will be legally binding upon the parties.

The entire procedure, and any documentation arising therefrom, will be confidential and treated as "without prejudice" and non-disclosable in any subsequent proceedings in the event of a failure of the parties to arrive at a settlement.

Subject to the preserving of limitation periods, and of other urgent interim preservation proceedings, all legal or arbitration proceedings shall be withheld or stayed for the duration of the procedure or for a determined period. The procedure may be brought to an end at any time by written notice given by one party to the other.

5. Costs

Unless otherwise agreed, the neutral adviser's fee and the expenses of the procedure shall be shared. Each side will pay its own legal costs.

Draft Initiating Procedure for Settlement of Disputes by Means of the Supervised Settlement Procedure

AN AGREEMENT made BETWEEN

(1) . . . . .of . . . .
. . . ."the First Party".
(2) . . . . .of . . . .
. . . ."the Second Party".
(3 . . . .)of . . . .
. . . ."the Third Party".

RECITALS

1. The following dispute has arisen between the First and Second parties . . . .
. . . .
. . . .
. . . .
(identify and describe dispute briefly) [and the Third Party is the insurer
of the Second Party]

2. The First and Second parties wish to attempt to settle their dispute by means
of the Supervised Settlement Procedure ("S.S.P.") of the Chartered Institute
of Arbitrators (the Institute), which is described in a pamphlet issued by the
Institute.

NOW IT IS AGREED as follows:

1. The Management Representative of the First Party is Mr. . . . .
. . . .and the Management Representative of the Second Party is . . . .
[The Management Representative of the Third Party is Mr . . . .].

Each of the above persons ("the Management Representatives") is
authorised to represent respectively the First and Second party at the formal
meeting [in the case of the First Party by resolution of the Board of the said
First Party dated. . . . .
and in the case of the Second Party by the resolution of the Board of the said
Second Party dated . . . .]
and is authorised to compromise the said dispute(s).

2 The Formal Meeting shall take place at . . . .
(state address) within [28] days of the date of the signature by the last of the
parties to this Agreement to sign the same ("the effective date").

3. The information and document exchange shall take place within [14] days of
the effective date.

4.   The proceedings shall be conducted in the [English] language and all documentation or copy documentation to be produced for the purposes of the S.S.P. shall be in that language or accompanied by a translation into that language. All interpretation and translation costs shall be an expense of the S.S.P.].

5.   The Neutral Adviser shall be Mr . . . . of . . . . (address). The fees of the Neutral Adviser shall be an expense of the S.S.P. If called upon by one, or all, of the parties to provide a written opinion as to the merits of the parties' cases the Neutral Adviser shall produce this within [21] days of the close of the Formal Meeting.

6.   All negotiations and the compromise agreement (if any) shall be concluded within sixty days of the effective date, failing which the S.S.P. shall come to an end. The period of sixty days and all other time periods may be extended by agreement between the parties, including the Neutral Adviser.

7.   From the effective date until the S.S.P. shall have come to an end the parties undertake to withhold (or if proceedings have been commenced, not to prosecute further) any legal or arbitral proceedings with the exception of urgent procedural measures necessary to preserve their rights, of which the defending party and the neutral adviser must be informed.

8.1   Unless already in existence for the purposes of formal arbitration or litigation, all verbal statements made, or written documents, including the compromise agreement (until finally executed) coming into existence during the course of, and for the purposes of the S.S.P., shall be treated as having been made or brought into existence "without prejudice" shall be inadmissible for use in any legal or arbitral proceedings and shall be kept confidential between the parties and by the Neutral Adviser.

8.2   Each party shall serve on any non-party with whom he is in communication in relation to these proceedings notice that the proceedings are confidential and privileged in respect of any matter or thing related to these proceedings and that under no circumstances may any of the following persons be called upon or compelled to give evidence in any litigation or arbitration proceedings connected with the subject-matter of the S.S.P.:
   (a) Any expert or legal adviser or other officer, servant, or agent of any party;
   (b) Any witness for a party, whether an expert witness or a witness as to fact;
   (c) The Neutral Adviser.
   The required notice shall be accompanied by a copy of this clause of this Agreement.

8.3 Neither the parties, nor their witnesses nor their advisers, shall introduce, in any legal or arbitral proceedings whether or not arising from or connected with the subject-matter of the S.S.P.):

(a) Views expressed or suggestions made by either or both parties or by the Neutral Adviser pursuant to a possible settlement of the dispute (or any part of the dispute);

(b) Admissions made by either party during the S.S.P.;

(c) Proposals made by the Neutral Adviser;

(d) Indications of willingness by either party to accept settlement proposals made by any party, including the Neutral Adviser, whether expressed in open or "without prejudice" correspondence or other documents;

(e) Evidence of abortive draft settlement agreements.

9. The S.S.P. may be brought to an end at any time by the service of a notice in writing by either the First or the Second Party on all the parties and on the Neutral Adviser. Notice may be served by telex or facsimile transmission, or by pre-paid letter post and shall be effective from the time of despatch or posting.

10. The expenses of the S.S.P., including but not confined to the fees of the Neutral Adviser, the interpretation and translation costs, and the costs, if any, of the hire of the meeting place for the formal meeting, shall be borne equally by the First and Second parties, who may be required from time to time by the Neutral Adviser to advance in equal proportions sums by way of deposit to cover such expenses. All payments made by way of deposit shall be lodged with [the Neutral Adviser] [The Chartered Institute of Arbitrators]. The parties shall be responsible for their own legal costs.

11. [The Third Party (as insurer of the First/Second Party) executes this agreement only in order to indicate assent to its provisions.]

DATED ....19 ....

SIGNED on behalf of the First Party by ....
its duly authorised representative

SIGNED on behalf of the Second Party by ....
its duly authorised representative

SIGNED on behalf of the Third Party by ....
its duly authorised representative

NOTE: This form of agreement provides for two parties who are in dispute, together with an Insurer of one of the parties. It may be drawn to cover any number of parties who are involved directly, or indirectly, in a dispute.

© Chartered Institute of Arbitrators

Case Selection

In developing criteria for case selection, consideration should be given to the following non-exhaustive list of points:

1. What are the company's objectives or business interests regarding the dispute? Is accelerated resolution desirable or essential?

2. What issues, legal and factual, are involved?

3. Is there a need for technical or other expertise?

4. Is there any sensitivity relating to the issues or a need for confidentiality?

5. What discovery has occurred and what is necessary in order to assess the potential for loss?

6. Does delay serve the company's or the opposing party's interest?

7. Are there insurance coverage considerations?

8. Are there limitation problems?

9. Are there problems with witness availability?

10. Will the choice of the arbitration/litigation forum and governing law favour one party over the other?

11. What are the likely costs and prospects for success if the matter proceeds to trial?

12. Are there any issues of principle or precedent involved which require a public adjudication?

Index